—

GODS WITHIN

—

Edited by Michael Perry
and published by SPCK:

Deliverance: Psychic Disturbances and Occult Involvement

Gods Within

A CRITICAL GUIDE TO THE NEW AGE

Michael Perry

First published in Great Britain 1992
SPCK
Holy Trinity Church
Marylebone Road
London NW1 4DU

British Library Cataloguing in Publication Data
A catalogue record for this book is available from the British Library

ISBN 0-281-04595-X

Typeset by J&L Composition Ltd, Filey, North Yorkshire
Printed in Great Britain by
The Longdunn Press, Bristol

Contents

Preliminaries

I would like to express my:

gratitude to David my Bishop and John my Dean for granting me
study leave in which I have been able to prepare this book, and to my
colleagues in diocese and cathedral for covering my duties during my
absence;

thanks to the Churches' Fellowship for Psychical and Spiritual
Studies for enabling me to cross the Atlantic, and to Spiritual
Frontiers Fellowship International and the Academy of Religion and
Psychical Research for giving me a place at their annual conferences
for 1991;

gratefulness to numerous librarians, and especially to Roger Norris,
whose enthusiasm and co-operation enabled me to consult many
more books on this subject than I would otherwise have thought
possible;

appreciation (alphabetically) to Eileen Barker, William Bloom, Hill
Brown, Wesley Carr, Peter Crick, James Fahey, Caroline Hardman,
Paul Heelas, Jim Hill, Andrew Perry, Kenneth Preston, Leslie
Price, Donald Reeves, Serena Roney-Dougal, Arnold Taylor, Willow,
and many others, known or anonymous, for discussions and correspondence which have both informed and corrected me and helped
clarify my thoughts (though I must insist that all remaining
errors and misapprehensions are – like Touchstone's Audrey –
ill-favour'd things, but mine own, and for them I take full
responsibility);

acknowledgements to those who own or control the copyright of
material I have quoted, especially to William Bloom for allowing me
to reproduce his statement of 'The Basic Ideas of the New Age
Movement' on pp. 33–36;

regrets that I have said nothing here about the relation of various
alternative and complementary medicine and therapies to New Age
ideas, my only excuses being ignorance and the need to limit one's
field if one hopes to say anything useful;

apologies for my inability to contort my prose style (which is shaky at best) or murder the grammar of the English language in order to avoid using the masculine pronoun;

love to Margaret and the family for bearing with me whilst this manuscript was in gestation;

and ***hopes and prayers*** that the result may be helpful to those who want to understand and react to the New Age movement.

Michael Perry
Durham
September 1991

1
Overgrown Gardens

As I turned somewhat apprehensively off Horseferry Road, through Elverton Street and into Greycoat Street to get to the Royal Horticultural Halls in Westminster, I wondered what I was in for, and how the experience would affect me.

It did not take me long to find out. Around the entrance there were several groups of people, presumably waiting for friends or taking a break between events. Nothing exceptional about them; a good mix of ages and sexes – not a pinstripe in sight, more sandals than lace-ups, but also very few in outlandish clothing or with outrageous hairstyles. An earnest-looking man in a dark grey shirt buttoned up to the collar was talking to a knot of younger folk. I caught a glimpse of the cross he was wearing round his neck and felt relieved that the Christians were in evidence. (There were also – though I did not discover it until later – some Evangelical groups pamphleting people on their way out and engaging in conversation wherever possible.)

Inside, I presented my ticket and went up into the hall to see what was on offer. The display of stands and exhibitions was breathtaking in its variety. There was a sweet and pervasive whiff of incense, with soft and soothing background music. Booksellers from Brighton and the Charing Cross Road, as well as from Ashby-de-la-Zouch and stations north, offering titles by the hundred – a bewildering array which would take a lifetime to read and absorb. Communities from Glastonbury to the north of Scotland, asking the punters to affiliate with them. Every kind of imaginable group, from astrologers to hunt saboteurs, and every conceivable kind of complementary medicine. There were radionics, iridiology, aromatherapy, colour and crystal therapy, Indian head massage, psychomassage therapy, self-improvement therapies to discover the God Within Us. Spiritual healers in white coats were passing their hands a few inches away from the bodies of their patients. Candles, crystals, incense, and jewellery on sale; royal jelly from Peking, aeolian chimes, tapes with

1

subliminal messages to help us eliminate stress, strengthen self-confidence, achieve sexual aliveness, or stop smoking. You could try out whatever kind of Yoga took your fancy. Rosicrucians, Spiritualists, Theosophists, astrologers, and Krishna devotees were all seeking adherents.

It seemed a little bit like the table described by Jesus the son of Sirach in the book Ecclesiasticus in the Apocrypha (31.12–21), at which the glutton was able to smack his lips and exclaim, 'What a feast!', reaching for everything within sight and jostling his fellow-guests at the dish. I wondered, however, whether what was on offer was nourishing goodness or mere junk food.

There was very little evidence of Christianity. I saw the grey-shirted man inside, and discovered that what he was wearing round his neck was not a crucifix but the ankh or *crux ansata* – the looped cross of the ancient Egyptians which was their symbol of everlasting life and which is nowadays much favoured by devotees of some schools of modern occultism to indicate their initiation. The only bodies which claimed to espouse Christianity were the Steinerians, the Swedenborgians, and the Greater World Christian Spiritualist Association. Admittedly, there were some stalls whose holders were trying to put the Church back to rights. A pamphlet alleged that St Thomas was the twin brother of Jesus. Another one proved (to its own satisfaction, at least) that Jesus was a vegetarian. He must have been; nobody who claimed divinity could have been cruel to animals (had the Creator forgotten what he was about when he made the carnivores?). Another pamphlet argued in bitter tones that the whole New Testament was a con built up by the followers of Paul who had suppressed the original message and gospel of Jesus, but that the Master had now returned to earth and to his Christhood, and had given back to humanity the original message which he had entrusted to a group called the Followers of the Way, from Kew Gardens.

And the crowds – bustling activity, swirling masses of people around the whole place, every day. I found it difficult to believe the friend who had told me beforehand that I should find the whole thing a 'paper tiger', with hardly any evidence of many people being involved, or of any real interest in the various subjects on offer.

Besides the stalls, and presentations of music and sacred dance, there were lectures and workshops. I went to several of them, but I did not always stay until the end. When the lecturer began to tell me that I could increase my mind power by breathing through my left nostril at dawn and my right one at dusk, according to the principles of prana yoga, I decided it was time to go. It was one thing keeping an open mind, but when my brains were in danger of falling out through the hole,[1] I reckoned I had had enough.

The whole scene in the Horticultural Halls seemed like a monstrously overgrown garden of the spirit, wild rather than cultivated. What had I come in to? What was going on there?

The Halls were the venue for the Fifteenth International Festival for Mind/Body/Spirit, a five-day event and the chief annual showpiece of the New Age movement. What, then, is this 'New Age movement'? And why was I studying it?

The second question first. I had been granted a few months' study leave, and thought it might usefully be spent in a more detailed examination of the New Age movement and of Christian responses to it. 'New Age' I had heard of from time to time, and New Age books and magazines had been crossing my desk more and more frequently in recent months and years in my capacity as Editor of a journal known as the *Christian Parapsychologist*, published by the Churches' Fellowship for Psychical and Spiritual Studies (of which more anon).

If my observations at the Mind/Body/Spirit exhibition were anything to go by, there are many people around today who are looking for a spiritual home. They have not found it (for various reasons) in the mainstream Christian churches. Many are looking for healing – the plethora of complementary therapies at the Exhibition was eloquent testimony to that. Many realize there is a relationship between spirituality and healing, but are puzzled as to what that relationship precisely should be. In the words of that rather sentimental Victorian evening hymn,

> ... some are sick, and some are sad,
> And some have never loved thee well,
> And some have lost the love they had.[2]

The movement was bringing different reactions out of Christians of different sorts. The more fundamentalist of the Evangelicals seemed to show anything from mild hysteria to frank paranoia. There were other places (like St James's Church in Piccadilly) which had seemed to me to have over-reacted in false guilt against the fundamentalists' venom, and were in grave danger of embracing the whole thing with something bordering on uncritical enthusiasm. Archbishop Robert Runcie (whilst he was still at Canterbury) had been attacked in some quarters after the 1989 Festival of Faith and the Environment around his cathedral. As a result, when he was addressing the conference of Senior Evangelical Anglican Clergy on 14 November 1989 he turned his attention to the claims of the New Age movement. He described it as a mix of eclecticism, mysticism, and syncretism, arising in reaction against the materialistic scepticism of so much of today's society, and called on Christians to take it seriously, in a 'spirit of engagement rather than of condemnation'. That (apart from a superabundance of words ending with '-ism') seemed to me to be the right way of going about it. The New Age movement needed a critical assessment. Was its argument with Christianity an indication that we were not stressing the right things in our presentation of the faith? Or was it that we had got some of our doctrines out of proportion in relation to others? Or did we need to change things, if we were to make Christianity attractive to those who had forsaken it for something which seemed to me to be distinctly second-rate as a faith on which to base the way I lived my life? And, if changes were being demanded of Christianity in order to make it more attractive to those who had abandoned it, we needed to be very sure indeed what was negotiable and what was not negotiable in this whole area.

But what *is* this New Age movement? Surely it cannot only be the kind of gentle battiness which I have just described at the Mind/Body/Spirit exhibition? There must, surely, be more to it than that? Philip Seddon of the Selly Oak Colleges describes it as 'a spiritual movement of powerful proportions, analogous to the Renaissance or the Enlightenment'.[3] Whilst I was in London, I had a lunch-time discussion with Dr William Bloom, the Director of the programme called 'Alternatives' that is hosted by St James's Church, Piccadilly. The exhibition, he said, was the froth on the top of the New Age movement, and ought not to be taken too seriously by those who are examining the underlying material. To do so would be about as fair as judging Roman Catholicism on the basis of looking at Mediterranean peasant superstitions.

We are, so the claim goes, at the threshold of a new age, and as the twentieth century draws nearer to its close, we shall hear more and more about it. Even now, once we have been alerted to its characteristic terms and 'buzz-words', we shall find references to it cropping up all over the place, particularly in journalistic articles about the way people are thinking and acting nowadays.

Some of the concerns of New Agers are the concerns of all of us.

For instance, there can be very few of us nowadays who are not worried about the environment and the future well-being of Planet Earth, bombarded as it is by the chemical and radioactive filth that the thoughtlessness and greedy folly of the human race has inflicted upon it. A concern for the earth and the environment is not specifically New Age; but the way in which New Agers think about the earth is not necessarily the same as the way in which Christian theology has thought about it. For that matter, the way in which Christians have thought about the environment and treated it in past centuries is not necessarily the right guide to how they ought to be thinking and acting today. 'New occasions teach new duties', and there are times when God points us towards a discovery of fresh things about himself and his world. Sometimes, when this is happening, it takes an awful long time for the truth to dawn on Christians. When God has new insights for his people, they can be very tardy in recognizing them. Look how long it took, and what a struggle it was, before the slave trade was abolished. So we need to look afresh at the doctrines of creation, and of our duties towards the created order, if we are to be at all responsible in our reaction to this aspect of New Age thinking.

Other 'New Age' ideas are not immediately recognized as such because they use common terms but use them in a different way from the rest of us. We shall see later on in this book that the term 'human potential' is like this.

Yet other ideas have been around a long time, but they are being given a particularly New Age run for their money. This is true of ideas such as astrology and reincarnation. But then, many New Age ideas are like this. Very few of them are not familiar to people who have made a study of philosophy or the history of religious concepts. Most of them, like ecologically-friendly paper, are 100% recycled. Not that this worries their practitioners. Most New Agers find this a positive virtue, because they believe that we have lost an Ancient Wisdom – whether the wisdom of ancient Egypt, or of the lost continent of Atlantis, or of the druids or of the practitioners of witchcraft. They believe there is a perennial philosophy within such lost systems that we need to rediscover for our souls' health.

Some New Age terms, however, *are* new (well, *relatively* new; whoever it was who wrote the book called Ecclesiastes, in the Old Testament, reckoned that there was nothing new under the sun, and he had a good point). For instance, there is 'channelling', and there is the idea that we are about to enter the 'Age of Aquarius'. And even here, the ideas of astrology are pretty ancient, and the word 'channelling' is only a new word to describe a phenomenon that is at least as old as the prophets of ancient Israel or the oracle at Delphi.

So, where did all these ideas come from, and how do they hang together? The first thing to note is that they are not all meant to 'hang together'. We may use a term like 'The New Age Movement', but it is not really a movement at all. At any rate, it is not a movement in the sense that we might use the word when, for example, we talk about the 'Scout movement'. The New Age is not an organization or a church or a denomination. If it is a 'movement' at all, it is more like a movement of thought, such as the romantic movement of the eighteenth century. It is like a fashion in thinking or a way of looking at the world or a way of understanding our relation to the universe. So the various ideas we have already mentioned are not necessarily part of one great philosophical or religious system. Indeed, many of them are incompatible one with another, and no one person could stay sane and believe in all of them. They are simply ideas which can be related to a climate of thought which they find congenial. And it is a climate of thought which is very pervasive today – not only amongst those people who would consciously describe themselves as subscribing to New Age ideas. That is part of its subtlety and part of its challenge to the Christian system of thought. That is why the emergence of the New Age movement, though it may not explicitly be setting the agenda for the religious life of the world at the close of the twentieth century, certainly 'contributes to the context in which Christian ministers now have to work'.[4]

This means that, although we can trace some of the ways in which New Age ideas have come to be formulated, it is not easy to assess the New Age as a single and coherent whole. Some of its ideas can be looked at in isolation, but it is more a case of trying to identify recurrent themes. Those themes will point us to the way in which Christianity has dealt with the same issues in the past, to aspects of Christian theology which New Agers seem to have ignored, and to places where Christian and New Age ideas remain irretrievably incompatible.

As we do this, we must enter sympathetically into the thought-world of the people who hold New Age ideas. So often, when Christians begin to describe systems of thought with which they disagree, they present them in such a way that the reader finds it hard to believe that any sane person could hold the ideas which are being so cruelly lampooned. If I have done this in the introductory pages of the present chapter, I hope I shall not be accused of doing it in the rest of this book. I have too much respect for the people who hold New Age ideas, even when I disagree with them. Remember again the words of Robert Runcie about a 'spirit of engagement rather than of condemnation'. That is what I have tried to do. I have tried to get 'under the skin' of those who hold the ideas, and practice the life-styles, which I describe. I have tried to understand them, to see why their ideas are attractive, and where I can agree with them. Only then have I allowed myself to be critical of them from a Christian standpoint, and then I have tried to be reasoned and reasonable rather than shrill and condemnatory. After all, my aim is not to destroy people's way of understanding the universe and to leave nothing in its place. Rather, I want to bring them to a knowledge of Jesus, the Christ whose service is perfect freedom. I can only do this if I start from where they are, and then try to show them a 'more excellent way'. I hope they, as well as convinced Christians and those who are simply curious as to what the New Age movement is all about, will read the following pages in that spirit.

2
Towards 2000

The year 2000 is a potent symbol. We may expect to hear more about it the closer it approaches.

It is easy to scoff. After all, there is no *real* significance in the year 2000. The twenty-first century does not begin until 2001, and in any case, if the beginning of the era was supposed to coincide with the birth of Jesus of Nazareth, we have long known that the date of that event has been miscalculated by a number of years. And why 2000? Because we have ten digits on our two hands, and ten toes apiece, we use a base of 10 for our enumeration. Had we used a base of 12, a more sensible and divisible number, then the year we now know as AD 1728 (1728 being 12 to the power of 3) would have marked the end of the first millennium, and nobody would have been at all excited about the approach of the year we now call 2000.

But symbols speak to us at a level which is deeper than that of logic and rationality, and as this present millennium draws to its close, it is not surprising that many people are taking stock of where the human race has got to, and what are its future prospects.

The idea that a New Age is about to be ushered in is not primarily astrological, but astrologers lend it strong support, and it is astrology which has lent it the name 'Aquarian'. The heavens are divided by them into twelve segments, each associated with its particular sign of the Zodiac. The earth's axis slowly changes its direction in space, so that the position of the sun in relation to the stars is not the same on the same day in succeeding years. The segment in which the sun rises at the spring equinox gives its name to the astrological age, and it takes just over two thousand years for this equinoctial precession to move us from one sign of the Zodiac to the next.

The age of Taurus the Bull began around 4000 BC, the traditional date on which Adam was expelled from the Garden of Eden. Aries the Ram followed in 2000 BC (Abraham's attempted sacrifice of his son Isaac [Genesis 22], prevented by the discovery of a ram in a thicket). Pisces the Fish has characterized the Christian era so far.

On this view, it is a significant coincidence that the earliest symbol of the Christian faith was derived from the acronym I-Ch-Th-U-S, the Greek word for 'fish', standing for 'Jesus Christ, God's Son, Saviour'. But the age of Pisces is nearly over, and the age of Aquarius the Water-carrier is about to dawn. Estimates vary as to when this will happen. One school puts it as 1 April 1995, when the planet Uranus enters its own sign of Aquarius,[1] but most authorities put it later, some as late as well into the twenty-first century.

Be that as it may, the New Agers claim that the Aquarian era will be very different from its predecessors. In this, they have the support of C. G. Jung, who, over thirty years ago, was writing about

> changes in the constellation of psychic dominants, of the arche-
> types, or 'gods' as they used to be called, which bring about, or
> accompany, long-lasting transformations of the collective psyche.
> This transformation started in the historical era and left its traces
> first in the passing of the aeon of Taurus into that of Aries, and
> then of Aries into Pisces, whose beginning coincides with the rise
> of Christianity. We are now nearing that great change which may
> be expected when the spring-point enters Aquarius.[2]

It is possible to see the Age of Aries as having been the age of the Father and the high-water mark of patriarchal religion, whilst the age of Pisces was the age of the Son, when institutional Christianity reached the zenith of its power. On this view, the stagnant Age of Pisces will soon give way to streams of living water, and, in the Age of Aquarius, the water-carrier will let the contents of his pitcher flow unchecked, and the freedom of the Spirit will burst all the constrict-ing dams of organized and hierarchical religion.

Certainly the mood at the end of this century is very different from that of a hundred years ago. Then, the British Empire was at the peak of its powers and Queen Victoria had reigned for more than sixty glorious years during which Progress (with a capital P) had continued unabated and Science (with a capital S) had solved all but a few tiresome little problems, which the opening years of the forthcoming century were going to resolve without much difficulty. The sense of optimism was legitimated by the theory of Evolution. The hymn by Addington Symonds (1840–93) expressed it perfectly:

> These things shall be! A loftier race
> Than e'er the world hath known, shall rise

9

With flame of freedom in their souls
And light of science in their eyes.

They shall be gentle, brave, and strong,
To spill no drop of blood, but dare
All that may plant man's lordship firm
On earth and fire and sea and air.

That was included within the hymn-book *Songs of Praise* in 1925. Who would dare ask a school or congregation to sing it nowadays?

The nineteenth-century myth of invincible progress was shattered into smithereens by the carnage in the trenches of the Somme front, and any remaining shards of it were disposed of when the war which followed the war to end war came to its nuclear close. The explosions of 1945 destroyed not only Hiroshima and Nagasaki, but the illusions of a whole generation. Since then, technology has been seen as bane as much as blessing, the promise of cheap nuclear energy has exploded like the reactors of Chernobyl, and a world weary of wars lurches towards the end of a century during which not a year has passed without some bloody conflict in some part of the globe leaving poverty, hunger, disease, and destitution in its wake. The ozone layer has been punctured, the rain forests destroyed for the sake of fatter Sunday newspapers, and there are those around who can claim with some degree of justification that Ben Elton's satirical novel *Stark* is right, and the ecosystem of the whole globe is in terminal decline. When the twentieth century dies, who will mourn its passing?

There is a widespread feeling that we have got things wrong, and that we need to try again, in a different way.

The book which has been most influential in spelling out that new way is *The Aquarian Conspiracy* by Marilyn Ferguson. (For details of this and all the other publications referred to in this book, see the Bibliography.) It took a mere eight years from its publication in 1980 to sell its first half million copies, which for a non-fiction work of close on 500 pages takes some doing. Marilyn Ferguson is the publisher of *Brain/Mind Bulletin*, which covers humanistic medicine and such subjects as memory, learning, creativity, and the physics of consciousness. Her book was subtitled *Personal and Social Transformation in the 1980s*. It is exuberant in its verbosity, and written in that kind of enthusiastically breathless style that gives the whole book a sense of exciting immediacy and its readers a feeling of being let into secrets about a new movement that will, very soon and with amazing rapidity, change the face of our whole world.

Ferguson's book charts a new paradigm. I remember, still with embarrassment, using that word 'paradigm' a little before it entered popular usage. I was in a TV studio and we were rehearsing for a discussion programme. I had got well into the swing of things, and my words were pouring forth like the pen of a ready writer, when, trying to be cleverer than was for my own good, I let fall the fatal word. The interviewer immediately said, 'Paradigm? What do you mean by that?' I was arrested in mid-flow, my mental processes froze, and, speechless, I cast around helplessly for what seemed like a silent age. The producer put me out of my agony by calling 'Cut!' and suggesting that we had rehearsed for long enough. But I determined never to use that word again without some explanation.

Marilyn Ferguson tells us exactly what she means by the term. A paradigm is

> a framework of thought (from the Greek *paradigma*, 'pattern'). A paradigm is a scheme for understanding and explaining certain aspects of reality ... A paradigm shift is a distinctly new way of thinking about old problems ... Einstein's Special Theory of Relativity formed the new paradigm that superseded Newton's physics ... Our understanding of nature shifted from a clockwork paradigm to an uncertainty paradigm, from the absolute to the relative. A new paradigm involves a principle that was present all along but unknown to us ... By its larger perspective, it transforms traditional knowledge.[3]

New paradigms are not immediately and universally accepted, and there are rearguard actions which may continue for a very long time – look at what happened to Copernicus or Galileo. But eventually reality will be (all but) universally perceived from the new perspective, and succeeding generations will wonder how it was ever possible to think of the world in any other way. The disconcerting thing about the twentieth century is that even the new paradigms do not last very long – there are already scientists around who are telling us that there are realms where we have to say, 'Einstein doesn't work here any more'.[4]

The paradigm shift which Ferguson charts is one which seeks to reverse the Gadarene stampede towards self-destruction that has characterized so much of what the twentieth century has thought of as progress. It began, typically, in California – 'a pluralistic environment friendly to change and experimentation' was a prerequisite[5] – and it needed people with 'affluence enough to be disillusioned with affluence',[6] but once it had started there, it moved East, not only to the rest of the United States, but also to the Old World.

Within this new paradigm, our minds are being transformed from the competitive to the collaborative mode. This can in turn heal and transform medicine, business, marriage, leisure, and scientific research programmes. 'Believing in a world of fixity, we will fight change; knowing a world of fluidity, we will co-operate with change'.[7]

Central to this whole paradigm shift, and a concept of which New Agers make a great deal, is the idea of the different functions of the two hemispheres of the human brain. Recent brain research has shown that in the majority of cases (some left-handed people are exceptions to the rule) the left hemisphere is more associated with logical and rational thinking, where words denote precise concepts and wholes are reduced to their sequential parts; whilst the right hemisphere is the intuitive side, where things are seen as wholes rather than as sequences, where words are poetical and symbolical and may have several layers of meaning, and where problems are solved by lateral thinking rather than by head-on confrontation.

In recent times, we have so overvalued the left-hemisphere activities that we find it hard to believe that the right hemisphere is useful for anything more than leisure activities. Music is all right for time off, but in the 'real world' mathematics is much more important. (Those who had to wrestle with the policies of the University Grants Council and its preference for technology rather than the arts will know this mind-set depressingly well.) Nothing could be more wrong. If we can only relax and become more bicameral – ambicephalous – we will become fuller people, and we may have some chance of building a better, more humane world. What is more, it will also be a more efficient world. Not only will we do good, we will also find ourselves doing well. And it is also much more healthy. Too many people use only half their brain:

> We isolate heart and mind. Cut off from the fantasy, dreams, intuitions, and holistic processes of the right brain, the left is sterile. And the right brain, cut off from integration with its organizing partner, keeps recycling its emotional charge. Feelings are dammed, perhaps to work private mischief in fatigue, illness, neurosis ... This fragmentation costs us our health and our

capacity for intimacy ... It also costs us our ability to learn, create, innovate.[8]

The new paradigm shows how it is possible for management and workplace philosophies to be human and humane, and still profitable (in fact, more profitable). In this new age, the National Product does not have to be nearly as gross as people imagine.

Marilyn Ferguson shows how this paradigm shift was already beginning to make changes throughout society by the end of the 1970s. But, when a paradigm is shifting, those who espouse the new ideas often imagine that they are isolated individuals swimming against the current. They are amazed when they discover how many people agree with them – sometimes as secretly as themselves. When they find this out, there is the feeling that they have been let in on a great secret conspiracy which will eventually change everyone's perceptions and ways of behaviour. Hence the title of the book. The conspiracy is largely hidden from its conspirators, and although there is a great deal of informal networking, there is no such thing as a great overarching organization. 'Because they aren't much for joining, the people involved in this inner search are hard to pin down statistically'.[9]

One of the more significant ways in which Marilyn Ferguson's new paradigm has taken over, and developed into New Age thinking, is in the area of human potential.[10]

In the middle of the century, psychology seemed to be stuck in a behaviourism for which the writings of J. B. Watson and B. F. Skinner were holy writ. Human beings were thought of like Pavlov's dogs. What mattered in psychology, and what could be studied, was overt behaviour; introspection formed no part of its brief. But in the early 1950s Abraham Maslow started a reaction against this kind of framework which at that time dominated American psychological schools. Looking back to Freud and, more especially, looking to Jung who had bidden us listen to our inner voices, he was more interested in inner states than behavioural manifestations. Concepts like creativeness, love, and responsibility became legitimate areas of concern to what were to become known as 'humanistic' psychologists. The processes of self-actualization and growth could once more be studied. Even metaphysics and mysticism were allowable topics of consideration.

Eventually, under the influence of Anthony Sutich, this led to a 'transhumanistic' psychology (the term was soon replaced by the word 'transpersonal') that saw as proper objects of study 'ultimate human capacities and potentialities and their actualization' such as 'self-transcendence, unitive consciousness, peak experiences, ecstasy, mystical experience, awe, wonder, ultimate meaning' and a host of other mind-expanding possibilities.[11] Transpersonal psychology was right in the thick of the territory formerly reserved for religion, and religious experiences were being studied by those academic psychologists who were touched by the new movement (which, obviously, was – and still is – very far from including all students or teachers of the discipline).

It was heady stuff, and an exciting time. In the psychedelic sixties there were experiments with the triggering-off of religious or mystical experience by the use of drugs; but as that avenue began to close, the interest moved East to physical, spiritual, mystical and meditational methods of achieving the same kind of illumination that the Timothy Leary generation had been seeking through lysergic acid derivatives such as LSD. The age of the Maharishi was upon us. People wanted to see just how far humans could go towards experiencing the transcendent; how body, mind, and spirit could be explored and integrated. Suddenly everything was a legitimate avenue for enquiry – from acupuncture to the *I Ching*, from Transcendental Meditation to the Tarot. Experience was everything, and it did not greatly matter whether we were delving into archetypal human concerns or tapping into a Great Universal Reality. Human potential was seen as vaster and more exciting than it had ever previously been imagined. The human potential movement was shading into what Nevill Drury terms 'its more visible but less discerning counterpart'[12] – the New Age movement.

In a more open and pluralistic religious setting like that of the late twentieth century, and in the wake of the anti-establishment counter-culture which began to emerge from the 1960s onwards, old, imposed, belief systems like Christianity were at a discount. There were those who exercised their choice by following gurus whose treatment of them was a great deal more authoritarian than that of any of the established belief systems they had rejected, and we had the unhappy spectacle of the Jonesville suicides and the forcible 'deprogramming' of Moonies and Scientologists.

Others, however, saw the new situation as one where they could 'do their own thing', become spiritually self-reliant, and explore the reaches of human potential in ways which were eclectic, syncretistic, and highly idiosyncratic. In this search, the aim is

14

that we should all endeavour to learn ways of tapping the sacred potential which is latent within our being ... The task for each of us is to rediscover the spiritual and universal in the everyday experience. This then becomes very much a personal quest, our own individual journey of the spirit. During our lifetime this may lead us along many different paths and through the company of many other guides and teachers ... [but] if the process is to be a journey of self-discovery, each of us should endeavour to awaken our spiritual potential in the most instinctual ways we can find, allowing the sacred to rise up from within our inner depths rather than submerging ourselves in imposed belief systems.[13]

This has its remote background in Dale Carnegie's *Power of Positive Thinking*, but the idea of human potential now began to be developed in ways which emphasized the latent divinity within humanity – gods within all of us. Shirley MacLaine, the American actress and spokeswoman for much New Age hype west of the Atlantic, tells her audiences that she is God, but that does not mean that we are not; indeed, we can only see that she is God if we realize that all of us are God, too.[14] That is a recurring refrain wherever the New Age takes up the theme of human potential, and it came over loud and clear in many of the presentations at the 1991 Mind/Body/Spirit Festival. Look, for example, at some of the lecture and workshop titles:

The intuitive road to the God within

Practical exercises for healing mind and body

Awakening spiritual and mental powers: energy mastery

Useful hints for the truly magnificent

Mind development for the New Age

How to prepare yourself for the acceleration of consciousness

Awakening your intuitive vision.

Or, on a lecture tour of England and Ireland, under the aegis of the Fellowship of the Inner Light, by Paul Solomon, billed as 'one of the most dynamic and insightful teachers in the modern human potential movement', the following subjects were to be covered:

Self-Love, Self-Worth, and Self-Esteem

The Way That is Certain to Prosperity

How to be Your Own Best Friend.

The 'meditation sanctuary' at the Mind/Body/Spirit Festival was provided by a couple of 'Pure White Light Therapists/Teachers' who put copies of their leaflet there, which proclaimed that

> our aim is for live awareness of personal self healing achieved by recognizing YOU ARE THE LIGHT ... Allow yourself the thought 'I am the Light' ... Maintain the Joy and Brilliance in that Oneness and be aware of your body. Know that you are the centre of that Light ... Because you are the *centre of this Light* you maintain LIVE AWARENESS of its Presence in every day activity by opening your eyes, bringing that Light into the world.

At one of the Festival workshops we were advised, without any apparent awareness of the fact that Emile Coué's phrase had been lampooned ever since his death over sixty-five years ago, to repeat to ourselves each morning the words 'Every day, and in every way, I am getting better and better'. And nobody appeared to find it funny. Or again, Neil Irwin suggests that we should meditate regularly on the phrase, 'I relax and surrender to the infinite light, love, wisdom and power of my higher self'.[15]

Miriam Simos, a wiccan who writes under the name of Starhawk, emphasizes that it is our self rather than any outside authority who has to discover and recognize whatever spiritual truth we are to live by:

> We are the Goddess: We are each part of the interpenetrating, intercommunicating reality that is All ... We need to win clear of the belief that only a few individuals in history have had a direct line on truth; [the belief] that Jesus or Buddha or Mohammed or Moses or Freud or Werner Erhard know more about our souls than we do. Certainly, we can learn from teachers, but we cannot afford to give over our power to direct our lives. A feminist religion needs no messiahs, no martyrs, no saints to lead the way. Instead, it must validate us in discovering and sharing our experiences, inner and outer. Its goal should be that impossible task of teaching ourselves – because we have no models and no

teachers who can show us the way – to become human, fully alive with all the human passions and desires, faults and limitations, and infinite possibilities.[16]

What is the purpose of all this? Is it ego massage? Is it an attempt to win disciples by flattering people into hearing what they long to be told, but could never have reasonably expected to hear? Or does it speak to the marginalized and give them the message of hope which their experience of life so far, and their exposure to religion so far, has all but beaten out of them? In particular, does the feminism of Starhawk and many another New Age teacher speak the liberating word to women, whose contribution to religion in recent centuries has been so devalued as to make them feel that they are unacceptable to the God either of the Christians or of the Moslems?

The human potential movement certainly sees itself as a powerful force for healing, and healing is high on the New Age agenda; and who is to say whether healing the hurts of the body or healing the hurts of the soul is the more important? We know enough already about psychosomatic effects to be sure that the healing of the soul is interconnected with the healing of bodily ailments. Cancer is not entirely a physical disease; it seems as if it can strike selectively where there is mental stress and it can be arrested by non-physical means. Not always, perhaps not often; but in enough cases to make us realize that body and mind are very closely interconnected and if we can affirm a person's worth as a human being we may be able to affect his chances of surviving a disease which is usually fatal.

Steven Levine writes of a woman who was very ill with advanced cancer, who went to a Zen master to ask about healing. Expecting to be told to go along some new spiritual path, she was surprised to be told by him, '*You* are the path!'. She began to attend meditation sittings, and after about three months, a sense of ease began to emerge. 'She trusted each step towards fullness, attuning to the subtle whispers of the heart, cultivating a healing awareness that received the moment in mercy, and allowed change instead of forcing it'.[17]

Lowell Streiker, commenting as a Christian on New Age healing, writes,

When I look closely at the table of probable causes and New Thought cures, when I read between the lines, I do not find several diseases with an appropriate cure for each, but a single malaise and a single prescription. In sum there is one problem – not loving oneself – and one solution – loving oneself. All the affirmations say one and the same thing: I am an expression of the divine life. I am worthy. I choose to accept and enjoy myself. Meditating on such sentiments, repeating them again and again, and offering them to God in prayer can change attitudes, patterns of behaviour, and circumstances.[18]

It is when it comes to eradicating illness and suffering that Streiker begins to express doubts. In India, what conquered typhoid, cholera, and smallpox was not positive thinking or meditation or chanting, but such rational approaches as sanitary engineering and vaccination. There is no one single and simple answer to a very complex question.

But it is still true that self-affirmation has an enormous power, and New Age has latched on to it to great effect. Half a century ago, Dietrich Bonhoeffer in Hitler's Germany was warning Christians that they would have to learn to live in a new world 'as if God did not exist'. The New Age seems to be one where humanity is being bidden to take the place of God. Lecturing at the Mind/Body/Spirit Festival on 'Where is God in the 1990s?' Soozi Holbeche said that many people felt today as if life was falling apart, and they wondered why God was letting it all happen. Perhaps this is exactly what was *meant* to happen; species are lost because their evolutionary cycle is over, and the hole in the ozone layer is an opening for us into another world. In a time of major planetary change, we need to wake up and look around us, and affirm our own power and our own potential. Energy has been coming into the earth for the last ten or fifteen years, and it will move the human beings on this planet from a self-conscious state to a cosmically conscious one. This may make us feel emotionally vulnerable, but we should hold on, and not be afraid. We are in the birth-pangs of a New Age. We can do anything, so long as we do not fear.

Where, then, is God for Soozi Holbeche? Everywhere! But he keeps out of sight and does not interfere – like a good parent caring for his children. Life, says Holbeche, is like a self-service restaurant; it is no good waiting to be served. We have to get up and help ourselves. We have access to our own inner wisdom as well as to our angel guides, but we must develop our powers or lose them. It is no good thinking that we have to wait until we are perfect. We must realize that we are perfect now. We were born perfect. We have to trust our own feelings and go ahead in faith.

Parts of this sound a little like the Christian message, but it is without any real conception of God. God has disappeared like the Cheshire cat, leaving only an ethereal smile behind. In the words of Lesslie Newbigin, 'there is only, in the background, the shadowy figure of Reality, whatever he, she, or it may be. Firmly in the centre is the self and the quest for personal salvation. And the self remains, in the end, alone in an unknown and unknowable world.'[19]

Human potential is not all that the New Age is about, but it is an important point of entry. We can already see that when we talk about the New Age, we are not dealing with a monolithic organization or with a single set of mutually consistent beliefs, but with a whole variety of ways of looking at the world towards the end of the second millennium. If it is a 'conspiracy', it is a remarkably ill-organized one! New Age ideas are linked by shared concerns, though the people who share them do not all reach the same conclusion. This is true of other themes which characterize 'New Age' thinking.

In the next chapter we will look at some of them and see how they fit into the general picture; and we will also look at a few significant publications and organizations which spread the New Age message.

3
Within the New Paradigm

In our opening chapter we described the 'presenting symptoms' of New Age involvement, as they were seen in all their obviousness to a visitor to the Festival of Mind/Body/Spirit. Then we went on, in our second chapter, to see that behind all this there lies a paradigm shift in the way in which people in the late twentieth-century Western world see themselves. Many people have latched on to a particular school of psychology which deals with human potential. They do so because they feel they have been missing out in life, and the 'human potential' teaching tells them that they do not need to be in this position. They have a birthright as members of the human race, and up to now nobody has told them about it. They grew up depotentiated, deskilled, and devalued, when all the time they ought to have been affirmed, led on, and fulfilled.

The concept of a latent and largely unrealized human potential legitimated a mass of philosophical and religious ideas about human nature – a shift in the self-consciousness of the human race, at any rate in the developed areas of the world. Most of these ideas had been around for some time, but it seemed at last that their moment had arrived. They have led to a proliferation of what we have called 'presenting symptoms' – to the popularity of beliefs about reincarnation or channelling or the intrinsic divinity of humanity; to the practice of dowsing or the use of the Tarot or *I Ching*, or to any one of a plethora of complementary techniques for discovering one's higher self or one's spiritual destiny. As Lowell Streiker points out, we need to

> note the pattern, for it runs through most New Age manifesta-
> tions: Individuals feel bereft of power, meaning and purpose.
> Traditional institutions and accustomed beliefs and mores seem
> inadequate and boring. Suddenly there arises on the horizon or
> within one's consciousness or in one's dreams or in the presence
> of a stranger or in the words of an arcane text an answer, the
> answer, the only possible answer.[1]

What, then, are the basic concepts which arose as the human potential movement transmuted into the New Age? We will look at some of them in this present chapter. Then, after a closer look at some particular manifestations of ideas which seem to run through a great deal of New Age thinking, we can return once more, in our closing chapter, to those basic concepts, and see what challenges they pose to Christian faith, and how the challenges might be met.

1. Free the spirit

In the Aquarian age, the human spirit must be free. No longer can we be told what to believe. No longer must we be in bondage to a hierarchical religion. Hugh de Cruz campaigns from an address in the Canary Islands for a 'New Age Universal Christianity without Religion' and tells his readers that 'you owe it to your God to stay away from organized institutionalised man-made "religion" because the Kingdom of Heaven is within you'. His material is not likely to be taken very seriously by the churches, but Dr William Bloom (whom we met in Chapter 1) is in a different league. According to him, the major problem of civilization

> has been the repression of our spirituality ... We have been subject to religions and churches which allow only one kind of belief or approach to the divine unknown ... The New Age phenomenon [is] the visible tip of the iceberg of a mass movement in which humanity is reasserting its right to explore spirituality in total freedom. The constraints of religious and intellectual ideology are falling away.[2]

In the New Age, we have to discover for ourselves what speaks to our condition, and follow the free spirit wherever it leads us. Pluralism is not simply a description of the current religious scene; it is a virtue in itself. So 'dogma' is a highly pejorative word and is used to denigrate the teachings of any established religion, and of Christianity in particular.

Truth is to be found, not in dogmatic propositions, but intuitively in the process of exploring a spiritual path. It is, probably, not even objective; it is whatever plucks the answering chord in ourselves. So,

> in the new paradigm 'truth' often appears only in quotation marks; one winks when one says the word. At least some

adherents of the new paradigm for thinking hold that Truth is not the discovery of the one correct (or most adequate) language for identifying real things, assessing their relative value and defining their relationships. Rather, truth, if the word has any meaning at all in the new paradigm, refers to useful ways we might wish to relate to the variety all around us; truth is learning the different language of things as they appear from different perspectives and within different experiences.[3]

If this be the case, then it is quite in order for there to be an eclectic borrowing from whatever traditions seem to speak to our condition. If our various borrowings are mutually inconsistent, or if what one person believes is formally inconsistent with what another person believes, it is not ultimately important. There is nothing sacred about the objectivity of truth. What *is* sacred is the inner experiential core which lies behind all the different religions, but which has been overlaid and obscured by the dogmatic systems which the theologians have reared upon it. In its essence this is a mysticism which, in the words of Aldous Huxley in his book *The Perennial Philosophy*, published as long ago as 1946, 'recognizes a divine Reality substantial to the world of things and lives and minds [and is allied to] the psychology that finds in the soul something similar to, or even identical with, divine Reality [and] the ethic that places man's final end in the knowledge of the immanent and transcendent Ground of all being'.[4]

If we are to discover this Perennial Philosophy, we must discover it for ourselves. We may need teachers and guides to put us in the way of it, but no church or dogmatic system can act as an intermediary. As in the Protestant Reformation of the sixteenth century, so now: we seek direct access to God, and organizations and systems only get in the way. It is a kind of DIY religion. We all

> now have the possibility of giving ourselves permission to re-negotiate our own most meaningful relationship with the living ground of Being ... To the extent to which the churches seek exclusive rights to contact with that which transcends day-to-day reality and consciousness ... they will be abdicating what should be their role: to help us reconnect ourselves *in our own way* [my italics] with our common Source as underlying reality.[5]

2. *Rediscovering ancient wisdom*

This leads many New Agers to a belief that our civilization has in recent centuries been going in the wrong direction and that we need to retrace our tracks and rediscover and reappropriate a more ancient wisdom. Herein lies one of the many paradoxes of the New Age movement. Although it may be termed 'New Age', it involves the rediscovery of age-old secrets. As the second millennium teeters towards its close, towards a wasteland of rampaging pollution in sea, earth, and ozone layer, the spiritual bankruptcy of Western technology is evident. If this is what Christendom has brought upon the world, then, say New Agers, we must find an alternative set of beliefs within which we can build a safer, gentler world.

The earth, as much as the people on it, needs to be affirmed to reach her full potential. She will not do this by factory farming and the intensive application of chemical fertilizers. The earth herself must be honoured, seen as holy, as a Goddess – Gaia – in her own right. New Agers believe that the old, patriarchal, religions can never do this. We need to go back behind them to an even older tradition, in which the feminine within deity is affirmed and the feminine values are seen as a way of salvation for the earth and her peoples. So we go back to the ancient religions of the Mediterranean world, or the religions of other lost civilizations of what we patronizingly call the 'primitive' world, or the Old Faith which succoured the people of this land before Christianity became the ruling system.

Other New Age groups believe that what we need to recover is an ancient occult wisdom, hidden for generations but now revealed once more to the human race in its hour of need. Gordon Melton points out how such 'ancient wisdom teachings' tend to emerge.[6] They begin by reports that someone has made direct contact with the guardians of a lost tradition in some remote part of the earth. Usually then they claim to have rediscovered the ancient texts which encapsulate this teaching. Frequently, however, no such texts exist and it is necessary for a special person to enter the occult realm in some paranormal way and secretly to be taught the traditions of this wisdom by disembodied Masters.

This certainly seems to have been the pattern in the case of Alice Bailey. Her name and writings are frequently extolled in the more metaphysical of New Age circles. She was a theosophist of the generation after Madame Blavatsky, and was responsible for twenty-five books of teachings totalling over 11,000 pages. In 1923, she founded the Arcane School, but this split into several distinct groupings after her death in 1949.

The schema propounded by Alice Bailey was a form of Theosophy akin to a Gnosticized or Neoplatonized version of Buddhism. It is a strange amalgam of monism and polytheism. It is monist in that she insists on the fundamental unity of matter and spirit, good and evil, human and divine. It is polytheist in that, despite this, there is a hierarchy of divine and semi-divine beings straddling the great gap between the ineffable Ultimate Unity and the multiplex world we inhabit. So: behind the phenomenal world there is the Lord Sanat Kumara. Under him there are three Buddhas, each of whom heads a hierarchy of Masters, who form the Great White Brotherhood. Within these hierarchies there are seven special Rays and a number of lesser beings. Master Jesus is one of the seven, but the Rays represent positions in the hierarchy, not persons, and the position once held by him is now occupied by Appolonius. Jesus has moved to take up the position of Master Maitreya and will one day – maybe very shortly – return to earth. Alice Bailey was the mouthpiece of Master Djwhal Khul, who dictated many of her books and who taught her the Great Invocation (see page 29 below). If this Invocation is used often enough, it will hasten the return of Maitreya to inaugurate a World Religion which will unite East and West and bring lasting peace to the earth. (Benjamin Creme issued a number of expensive advertisements in the national press in 1982 claiming that Maitreya was living within an immigrant community in East London and would soon be manifested in public by appearing simultaneously on every television screen in the world, but the phenomenon never happened, although Creme is still promoting a revised version of this scenario.)

All this sounds a strange farrago. It will be strange even to those many followers of New Age ideas who have not been initiated into it. It cannot be denied, however, that the more metaphysically inclined New Agers set great store by Alice Bailey's teachings, and the anthology of New Age writings edited by William Bloom and issued as a follow-up to the series of ITV programmes on the New Age in early 1991 was dedicated to Djwhal Khul.

The Bailey schema is the most widespread form of New Age metaphysic, but there are other options. Some groups believe that what the world needs is a form of Christianity which, in the early centuries of this era, was declared heretical and driven underground by a triumphalist orthodoxy, but which is now seen as the only true way for mankind. Such a system may be claimed as Essene or Gnostic or Templar, though its connections with what reputable scholars of those movements have discovered about them is often tenuous in the extreme.

This whole aspect of the New Age is described by William Bloom in the following terms:

> One of [the major characteristics of the New Age movement] is its honouring of all the esoteric religious traditions and of the mystic traditions of native peoples. A remarkable renaissance of the wisdom traditions is taking place, both those within the major religions and those of indigenous peoples. Within the major religions, for example, are the gnostic tradition of Christianity, the Qabalah of Judaism, Sufism in Islam, and Zen and meditation techniques of Buddhism. The native traditions include those of Celtic Europe – such as Wiccan and Druidism – north American Indians, Australian Aborigines and African medicine people. And there is a powerful rebirth of the female aspects of deity, as the Goddess resumes her crucial role in our lives.[7]

3. New Age paradoxes

But there are paradoxes.

1. One of them lies in the way in which some New Agers have exchanged what they have perceived as an undesirable spiritual captivity for a worse one – which they seem not to have perceived. They have allowed themselves to be dominated by an authoritarian guru and to believe that his every pronouncement is written in stone more lasting than that on which Moses received the Ten Commandments. Or they have abandoned one religion because they think it is too dogmatic and have taken on another philosophical system which enslaves them even more completely, and removes from them the capacity (and even the desire) for independent thought.

2. A second paradox arises from the realization that full human potential is reached only after sweat and tears, blood and toil. Most New Age followers are gentle people who believe that their chosen spiritual path can be attained by hard work and goodwill. There are, however, New Age methods of management training which are a great deal fiercer than that, and which are almost fascist in the harsh way in which their trainees are moulded. An acquaintance has described it as 'New Age with the jackboots on'.

So we get schools which promise

> a powerful, state-of-the-art goal-setting programme that works for the individual and the organization, [which] has the capability to establish strong, collective focus on goals and objectives. It ... has developed techniques which enable participants to identify and move past unproductive efforts, and to use their minds more effectively to create desired results without delay. These techniques create conscious, positive energy and turn apparent mistakes into moments of tremendous power.[8]

We might expect language like this in brochures of high-profile hard-sell business training seminars of the Old Age variety, but it does not seem to comport all that well with the movement which we have so far been describing. Yet it is a legitimate development of the human potential movement, it is marketed as 'Skills for the New Age', and it is included within a programme containing information about such familiarly New Age topics as the Planetary Mind, the Vibration of Love, and Channelling. 'The 80s', it goes on, 'were about taking responsibility and empowerment. The 90s will be about being powerful and actualizing that power in our world.'

3. A third paradox is that although the New Age propels us on a search for the ancient wisdom of primitive cultures, it also appeals for part of its validation to the latest insights of modern science. Twentieth-century physics has blown apart the billiard-ball, mechanistic, predetermined universe of Newton's day and replaced it by a universe which is a dance of insubstantial energy – except that energy is now realized to be the primal substance and therefore not insubstantial, but *more* substantial than the matter into which it agglomerates.

Werner Heisenberg discovered that at the subatomic level it was impossible simultaneously to measure the position and momentum of a particle except within strict limits, so that the more accurately one pinpointed the first, the less certain one could be about the second. That became known as the 'Uncertainty Principle', and dethroned the observer from his Newtonian position of Olympian detachment. The experimenter affected his observations by the very fact of observing them. The scientist is part of his data. From there we move on to the mind-boggling incomprehensibilities of quantum physics, in which particles move from one orbit to another without passing through the space in between (the term 'quantum leap' has become a real New Age buzz-word). In this realm, probability is a better guide to the likelihood of molecular interaction than fixed mathematics, and things which look as though they are impossible are in fact only seen as highly improbable.

All these ideas apply in their strict sense only to events at the submicroscopic level and ought not to be extrapolated beyond the confines of nuclear physics, but their supposed metaphysical corollaries are too tempting to ignore. The latest candidate for New Age canonization is chaos theory, in which the smallest input to a labile system can cause the most catastrophic results – the beating of the wing of a butterfly can affect the weather pattern of an entire continent.

The hologram has also been taken over by New Age expositors to legitimate ideas about the universe as a whole by using terms from modern science. Two coherent rays of light, when they impinge on an object in their path, produce an interference pattern which can be recorded on film. The film can then be used in order to create a three-dimensional image of the object. What is intriguing is that one does not need the whole film in order to recreate the whole object. Half of it will do, or a quarter, or only a tiny fragment. Admittedly, the detail is lost as the film area becomes less, but the object is still fully reproduced. That becomes the scientific fact on which our understanding of the whole universe can be based: 'The Universe is enfolded multi-dimensionally on itself. Like a hologram in which any single part contains a picture of the whole, so the Universe, although manifest in an infinite number of forms, is nevertheless contained holographically in any particle.'[9]

Some Christian apologists use Heisenberg, holograms, and related ideas (often without understanding them, and often as illegitimately) to argue that a spiritualized interpretation of the world is by no means inconsistent with the most up-to-date scientific theory. The point at issue for the moment, however, is simply that it is paradoxical that the New Age movement, which rejects the fruits of technology and seeks to regress to the primitive in its religious understanding, wishes at the same time to be up-to-the-minute in its use of arguments based on modern scientific discoveries.

4. *Cosmic optimism*

If human potential is limitless and there is a little bit of God within each of us, then we are responsible for our own spiritual progress and need neither God nor saviour outside of ourselves. Indeed, there is nothing to be saved *from*. Although New Agers recognize that there is plenty in the world which prevents their dream of a renewed cosmos from coming immediately into being, this fact is far from central to their philosophy. There are unenlightened people who hinder the coming of the great future, but it is enlightenment which is required rather than anything akin to what Christians would call repentance and conversion.

So there is an inherent optimism in New Age thinking. It is well expressed by Ruth Montgomery's 'guides' who tell us that

> the New Age has begun, but will not be fully recognized as such until the shift of the [earth's magnetic] axis has eradicated some of the evils of the present age. The earth will be swept clean of the beastliness and cupidity that now surrounds us, and will see the flowering of civilization in which the best of man's instincts are given full range.[10]

Note that sin and evil are seen as curiously external to mankind. They will disappear automatically, by the shift of the earth's axis, without the need for human intervention and certainly without the need for any radical reorientation of personality.

Most New Age teachers believe the transformation will be a little less automatic than that, and that human co-operation and effort will be needed if it is to come about. Maharishi Mahesh Yogi taught that if a certain percentage of humanity was to engage simultaneously in Transcendental Meditation, amazing powers would flow inexorably into the whole community and the New Age would have arrived.

There is a similar easy optimism in 'Triangles', which was begun by Alice Bailey as long ago as 1937 but is still being promoted. It is 'a network of concentrated thought and meditation. People link mentally to create triangles of light and goodwill as a world service ... Through this network spiritual energies of love and light can be released to help transform the climate of human thought and relationship.'[11]

The practice of synchronized meditation is a widespread New Age recommendation. It seems to be based on the premise 'that prayer at particular times and places has special power (e.g.) "to change the consciousness of our planet for the benefit of all living things"'.[12] This is not the same as the Christian concept of prayer; it locates the power of prayer in the person who prays and in the action in which he engages, whereas Christian prayer is an attempt to align the will of the person who prays with the will of God, in whose power alone it lies to grant the request.

The 'feel' of New Age is especially caught in the Great Invocation. This was originally composed by Alice Bailey for 'Triangles', and (as we have seen) was linked with her teachings about the Masters and especially with the idea that it would help Maitreya come to earth. It has of late been extensively taken up within the wider New Age movement, and has even been known to be used (in whole or in part) in inter-faith services, probably without its origin being realized:

> From the point of Light within the Mind of God
> Let Light stream forth into the minds of men.
> Let Light descend on earth.

> From the Point of Love within the heart of God
> Let love stream forth into the hearts of men.
> May Christ return to earth.

> From the centre where the Will of God is known
> Let purpose guide the little wills of men –
> The purpose which the Masters know and serve.

> From the centre which we call the race of men
> Let the Plan of Love and Light work out.
> And may it seal the door where evil dwells.

> Let Light and Love and Power restore the Plan on earth.

These basic ideas need to be fleshed out in actual examples of New Age teaching, and this we will be doing as this book continues. Where may they be found and studied?

As soon as you begin looking into New Age philosophy and practices, you will come across the term 'networking'. The New Age does not work like an organized multinational corporation, or like a religion with a centralized hierarchy and a set of credal standards. As we have seen, it is the name for an unco-ordinated medley of individual groups or movements or organizations or techniques or insights or practices, none wishing to unchurch any other, but all competing for attention. Networking happens through a number of published directory guides, but more through the pages of the innumerable magazines – often amateurly printed and of small or local circulation – which carry classified and display advertising.

These, typically, feature a number of 'core' New Age people and organizations, and a far larger number who might share New Age concerns and are looking for wider support, but who would not consider themselves to be New Agers. The rest would be some of the host of entrepreneurs who provide services, products, health foods, and the like. Perhaps the most significant of these magazines is *Leading Edge*[13] which is a widely-circulated glossy, describing itself as concerned with 'exploring the new perspectives of the 1990s in the arts, business, complementary therapies, ecology, health, science and spiritual awareness'. Networking also happens in shops – particularly in health food or earthcare shops, especially if (as often happens) they sell a few magazines or have a noticeboard.

Information about New Age teachings and concerns can also be obtained from the plethora of published books which are currently flooding the market. If your local bookshop has any section at all headed 'religion', you can be pretty sure that most of what it stocks will be of a New Age character rather than from orthodox or mainstream faiths. In itself this tells you something about the reading public's perception of the importance of New Age ideas, as well (sadly) as something about the average orthodox Christian's reluctance to buy books on his faith.

Particular places are highspots of New Age activity. They are places which have been recognized as holy, and which are therefore places of pilgrimage. Glastonbury is one, and Iona another. The holy island of Lindisfarne seems to have escaped by reason of its remoteness, and Stonehenge because of the efforts of the Department of the Environment to restrict access. Forres in north-east Scotland is the home of the Findhorn Community where ecologically-concerned New Agers are welcome for introductory stays.

Then there are organizations. St James's Church in Piccadilly gives room to 'Alternatives' which meets in the church on Monday evenings to hear a New Age presentation.[14] The Scientific and Medical Network[15] is not explicitly New Age, but links professionals who believe that the mechanistic and mainstream interests, both in medicine and more widely in science generally, do not tell the whole story. The largest New Age organization in the UK is the Wrekin Trust,[16] founded by Sir George Trevelyan in the early 1970s after his retirement from being principal of an adult education college in Shropshire (the Wrekin being a local hill in that county). This arranges a large number of residential conferences and one-day training events in all parts of the country, as well as guided pilgrimages to significant sites in Europe and the Holy Land.

The New Age was the subject of a six-part series on Channel Four television in early 1991, and a book of extracts from New Age writers followed the programme. Edited by Dr William Bloom as *The New Age: An Anthology of Essential Writings*, it is a very good introduction to the concerns and ways of thinking of New Agers. The best objective view of the whole field is to be found in J. Gordon Melton's *New Age Almanac*, a comprehensive volume of 496 pages with chronology, potted histories of various aspects and beliefs, biographical details of personalities, bibliographies and photographs. The only thing it lacks (conspicuously) is an index, and it is fuller on the American than the British aspects of the movement. But it is a mine of information, without which it would be almost impossible to be even reasonably well-informed about all the labyrinthine ways of the New Age.

To try to get the typical flavour of the movement, let me end this chapter by giving you (vicariously) three New Age experiences. The first is to engage in a typically New Age meditation; the second is to listen to Sir George Trevelyan lecturing. The third is to look at William Bloom's summary of New Age beliefs. By then we ought to have a feeling for what it is we are talking about.

1. In order to meditate, you will need to position yourself comfortably either in a chair or on the floor. Preferably make sure that your spine is upright and straight so that the *chakras* or seven mystic 'energy centres' of yogic teaching are in a line. You will need to still your left brain and allow your brain hemispheres to achieve a balance; this is best done by listening to taped music of a somewhat formless variety. You may find it useful to have a lighted candle, or a crystal, in front of you, on which you can centre. Now you are ready to begin your meditation. The following text shows the kind of mental journeys you will then be invited to follow:

> Feel your heart energies connect to the heart of the universe, the source of light and love; connect to the Sun, the central heart of our solar system; and draw the life force into your heart on the in-breath. Project feelings of love, joy, wealth and abundance outwards from your heart on the exhale. See your centre getting stronger and brighter with every breath. Know that the supply of love energy is infinite and the more you give the more you are

open to receive. Feel yourself a channel for LOVE – surrender to the Higher Power. Feel compassion and forgiveness for yourself and all others. Love yourself. Be yourself. Be natural.[17]

2. Typical of New Age teachers (if one who is so obviously his own man can be called 'typical' of anything) is Sir George Trevelyan, now in his eighties but still one of the most powerful speakers on the New Age circuit. In May 1991 he was talking to an audience which had come to hear him speak about 'The Rising Tide of Love'. According to my notes, these are a few of the things he said:

The 'I am' in you is a droplet of divinity in a bodily temple; a little piece of God. Life cannot die – that would be a contradiction in terms. You always were and you always will be. Earth lives are a training school for souls, and we are to expect a long series of them. None of all this is dogma that I am asking you to believe; dogma causes divisions among religions, each claiming to be the truth. No, what I am doing is offering you ideas which you can take or leave.

The earth is a living body, and God is the great creative Force, in everything. There are nine hierarchies of angels, and the tenth, a little lower than the angels but crowned with glory and honour, is Man. The purpose of the human race is that one individual human being after another, after countless lives, should wake up to the vision of what life on earth is really about. Our human freedom must not be violated; we must come to this realization without coercion. But when we come to that realization we shall know our own Godhood. The planet is going to be cleansed and a New Age will come. Death is nothing but the release from the necessary limitations of a soul enfleshed within materiality.

We have identified the Christ with Jesus, but in fact the Christos, the principle of love, was something which entered Jesus at his baptism and for three years inhabited that body, so that Jesus stepped back to give place to the Christ-principle. In our thinking, we have overloaded Jesus with a godhead-quality which is more than his soul can bear. He was only the vehicle whereby God entered the flesh of earth. The Second Coming is not the return to earth of Jesus but the enChristing of all of us.

The New Age will be the re-entry of the heart of God as a driving force of love flowing into a planet of freewill, and filling all things. When we overcome the greed and fear of the ego and become a heart-centre, the rising tide of love will flow. This rising tide of love will never be checked; the frozen misery of centuries is beginning to melt, and we are the ones who are destined to see this wonderful thing happen.

That should not all be taken literally. It is part poetry, part rhetoric. But it gives the feeling of the kind of things said to New Age followers by one who has been more influential (probably) than any other single person in the UK in the promulgation of New Age ideas, and therefore I make no apology for sharing this transcript of the notes of an hour's inspirational utterance.

3. Is it possible to describe the basic ideas of the New Age in a single statement? The following was prepared by Dr William Bloom of the St James's team, Piccadilly, for a conference arranged by the London School of Economics on 28 April 1990. The first half of it is printed in the form in which it appears on pages 12–14 of his book *Sacred Times*. (That book also contains New Age rituals for people who wish to celebrate births, marriages, and deaths but who cannot accept the truth of Christian teachings. For good measure, it adds suggestions for ways of celebrating the lunar and solar festivals.) I know no better summary of the ideas underlying the New Age movement, and I am grateful to Dr Bloom for so kindly allowing me to reproduce it in full.

The basic ideas of the New Age movement

[The basic ideas of the New Age movement] are not meant to be a box of beliefs – get in and stay in. They are meant as an open-ended scaffolding on to which we can hang our experiences, wisdom, and intuition. I produced this list in the Spring of 1989 and circulated it for criticism. I have made a few changes, but the major criticism was that the list did not catch the excitement and inspiration of our times. So, with the caution that the list is a dull representation of extraordinary realities, I hesitantly present it:

* All life – all existence – is the manifestation of Spirit, of the Unknowable, of that supreme consciousness known by many different names in many different cultures.

* The purpose and dynamic of all existence is to bring Love, Wisdom, Enlightenment . . . into full manifestation.

* All religions are the expression of this same inner reality.

* All life, as we perceive it with the five human senses or with scientific instruments, is only the outer veil of an invisible, inner and causal reality.

* Similarly, human beings are twofold creatures – with:
(i) an outer temporary personality and
(ii) a multi-dimensional inner being (soul or higher self).

* The outer personality is limited and tends towards materialism.

* The inner being is infinite and tends towards love.

* The purpose of the incarnation of the inner being is to bring the vibrations of the outer personality into a resonance of love.

* All souls in incarnation are free to choose their own spiritual path.

* Our spiritual teachers are those souls who are liberated from the need to incarnate and who express unconditional love, wisdom and enlightenment. Some of these great beings are well-known and have inspired the world religions. Some are unknown and work invisibly.

* All life, in all its different forms and states, is interconnected energy – and this includes our deeds, feelings and thoughts. We, therefore, work with Spirit and these energies in co-creating our reality.

* Although held in the dynamic of cosmic love, we are jointly responsible for the state of our selves, of our environment and of all life.

* During this period of time, the evolution of the planet and of humanity has reached a point when we are undergoing a fundamental spiritual change in our individual and mass consciousness. This is why we talk of a New Age. This new consciousness is the result of the increasingly successful incarnation of what some people call the energies of cosmic love. This new consciousness demonstrates itself in an instinctive understanding of the sacredness and, in particular, the interconnectedness of all existence.

* This new consciousness and this new understanding of the dynamic interdependence of all life mean that we are currently in the process of evolving a completely new planetary culture.

[So far the statement in *Sacred Times*. Dr Bloom continues:]

Essentially the New Age movement is concerned with individual spiritual experience. It is in many ways a liberation movement, seeking to free and to empower the individual's private experience of spiritual realities – freedom from religious dogma and authority, and empowerment in the face of a mainstream intellectual culture which at best patronises and at worst disdains spiritual realities.

New Age culture respects experience. It honours the divine in all life and is filled with enthusiasm for any path or tool that leads to and strengthens people in their experience of the divine. New Age culture believes that we live in an interdependent local and cosmic environment, and that for various reasons humanity as a whole is currently passing through a transformation of consciousness. This transformation is manifest in a new sense of personal divinity and in a new sense of the spiritual interdependence of all existence. This, in turn, is reflected in what is being recognised as a general paradigm shift away from a predictable Newtonian billiard-ball model of life to a more open-ended and intuitively understood model.

The New Age movement itself therefore demonstrates a wide spectrum of thought and approach. It is perhaps at its most intellectually respectable and acceptable when it speaks purely of the paradigm shift and reflects on the new insights from sub-atomic physics, from the new biology, from humanistic and transpersonal psychology, and from the new green awareness particularly including the concepts of deep and spiritual ecology.

At the other end of the spectrum, it is concerned with deep mystical experience, an experiential exploration of spiritual dimensions and an understanding of the esoteric dynamics of the universe. In its explorations of these areas, it places primacy on personal first-hand encounters and realisations. It is enthusiastic about all tools and paths which facilitate these realisations, but with profound reservations about any path which involves cultism or the loss of individual autonomy.

New Age culture particularly respects the tools and paths of the past and of indigenous peoples, paths which have in the main been repressed or ignored. New Age culture, therefore, is associated with a renaissance of the mystery and esoteric traditions; and New Age culture recognises that these traditions, whilst communicating in widely different symbols and myths, are describing the same essential spiritual truths and delineating the same esoteric maps. At the same time, the New Age movement recognises the phenomenal amount of contemporary inspirational and esoteric teachings that have appeared over the last century. (Some of it is rubbish.) All these teachings, both ancient and contemporary, not only give guidance concerning approaches to spirit, but also give counsel concerning living one's daily life. In particular it encourages people to take full responsibility for their conduct and attitudes, within the context both of personal growth and of an interdependent world.

Hand-in-hand with these teachings and spiritual techniques, New Age culture also embraces and stimulates those psychological approaches and techniques which work with spiritual experience. Where these new psychological approaches meet the traditional esoteric spiritual approaches is in the acceptance that every human is on a path and involved in a spiritual process involving transformation and the fulfilment of human and spiritual potential.

As in all affairs that involve large numbers of people, the New Age movement has both sages and idiots, saints and sinners, sincere and manipulative egos. In general, however, it demonstrates a high degree of social and ecological awareness; it demonstrates a particularly useful attitude in understanding that life can be led as a self-reflective process of growth and transformation; and it liberates spirituality from the confines of religious dogma and empowers direct personal experience.

Cultural	*Spiritual*
New Science	Pisces > Aquarius
New Psychology	Fuller incarnation of Cosmic Love
New Ecological Awareness	Humanity as 'successful' disciple
New Electronic Culture	New 'Group' Awareness
Global Village	Cosmic Interdependence
Transformation of consciousness	Transformation of consciousness
	Many new sources of Revelation
	+
	Renaissance of mystery, Esoteric and Indigenous traditions

NEW PARADIGM   +   NEW AGE

= NEW CULTURE

Now that we have an overview of the New Age movement, we will spend a few chapters looking at some of its more significant outworkings in greater detail. Then we shall be the better able to see it again as a whole, and return to a Christian critique of it all.

4

Mantic
Methods

To most people, the word 'mantis' conjures up the image of a particularly nasty little insect with its forelegs hypocritically folded as if in prayer; but the Greek word *mantis* meant a 'soothsayer', so the adjective 'mantic' means 'pertaining to divination'. Hence the title of this chapter.

There are many methods of divination which find favour with New Agers. Undoubtedly the most popular is the Tarot, though Nordic runes or the Chinese I Ching are also fairly widely used. Then there are methods like scrying in a crystal ball or reflective surface, dowsing with a pendulum or forked stick, reading the aura or deciphering a Kirlian photograph. Psychometry, or gaining impressions by paranormal means from handling an object belonging to the client, and the use of the ouija board or planchette, are more used by mediums than by New Agers; and there are innumerable other methods, from the interpretation of tea-leaves to palmistry, which belong more to old-fashioned fortune-telling than to New Age thought. But since the terms New Age and Age of Aquarius send our first thoughts to astrology, let us begin there.

1. Astrology

Hardly a newspaper or magazine nowadays dare appear without its regular astrological column. That in itself shows how many people like to look at what 'their' stars foretell. Whether they take any significant notice of what they find there, or whether they just look at it in an idle moment and for a giggle, is a moot point. It is a sobering thought, however, that astrology claims ten thousand professional practitioners and twenty million clients in the USA alone.[1]

But whatever else the newspaper horoscopes are, they are not serious astrology, and neither New Agers nor real astrologers regard them as more than pop pap. A genuine, as distinct from a newspaper, horoscope, takes so many data into consideration and has to be computed with such precision, that it is absolutely unique to the person or situation whose characteristics it is attempting to illuminate.

Real astrology is quite different from the compilation of newspaper horoscopes. William Bloom told me that it is an art which can only be properly appreciated from within the astrological community. Since I do not stand within that community, I can only offer comments as an outsider. But I *can* appreciate that it is seen by its practitioners as a sacred art, giving 'access to an intuitive perception of the workings and energies behind life'.[2]

It is based on a philosophy which sees the universe as a single organism within which all the parts are interconnected. Humanity is the link between earth and the heavens. If the moon can affect the tides and the sun the seasons, why should not the position of the planets affect the actions of human beings? 'As above, so below', say the astrologers; and if you suggest that the gravitational force or electromagnetic field of a planet could have very little effect on the behaviour of an individual, they are quite likely to answer that our receptors can be most incredibly sensitive, and that, moreover, modern 'chaos' theory, as developed by the theoretical physicists, tells us that the most massive of systems can be quite seriously affected by the tiniest of physical causes.

In any case, the effect need not be physical. It could be symbolic or archetypal, and the quality of a particular moment could impress itself upon a person or a situation and shape its outcome in surprising ways. Or maybe, taking up Jung's idea of synchronicity, and remembering that Jung was disposed to take astrology more seriously than his colleagues, we could say that

> the positions of the heavens at a particular moment in time, by reflecting the qualities of that moment, also reflect the qualities of anything born at that moment, whether it be an individual, a city, an idea, a company or a marriage. One does not cause the other; they are synchronous, and mirror each other.[3]

If this be so, then the positions of particular heavenly bodies could affect the behaviour of particular human beings, and large-scale movements of the earth in relation to the heavens (like the equinoctial sunrise moving into another segment of the skies) could cause large-scale and generalized effects upon the whole of human society (like the paradigm change which is heralding the dawn of the Age of Aquarius).

There are many different branches of astrology. The one with which most non-practitioners are most familiar is birth astrology. There is also horary astrology, where a question is asked, and the chart drawn up for the time of asking; and electional astrology, which can indicate the right time to begin an enterprise (a practice which became notorious during the Nancy Reagan years at the White House).

If you are worried that all of this involves a deterministic world in which Fate and the stars decree the future and we lose our freewill, have no such fears. The modern, New Age style of astrology is known as Creative rather than Predictional. During this century,

> astrology in the West has become increasingly concerned with the inner world, with psychology. Character delineation, the inter-pretation of the individual natal chart, has become central to the astrologer's practice ... This idea of the 'inner man', the greater or higher or deeper Self, towards which the lesser self can grow in wisdom and responsibility, is a commonplace nowadays in New Age circles ... The modern psychological astrologer reads character, our subjective reality, rather than destiny, our objec-tive circumstances, from the information on the natal chart.[4]

Or, to quote another recent astrological writer,

> predictive astrology is a bit of a misnomer because fate is something which we can each make for ourselves. All that one can do is to show the forthcoming trends and point out to the subject where things are going to flow along easily and where they are not. What he then chooses to do with his life is up to him.[5]

So a horoscope is a birthchart

> which describes a person's character and suggests areas of his personality which could grow and develop ... The purpose of learning astrology, therefore [is] to understand the innate character of a person, place, situation or enterprise and to follow its develop-ment and the way it interacts with others over a period of time.[6]

Not that all this is particularly new. W. F. Allen ('Leo') was teaching it at the turn of the century, and its roots go back to the very early days of astrology.

The same is true of what is termed 'medical' astrology.[7] The natal horoscope is believed to yield clues as to its owner's character and, therefore, to his predisposition to disease. This, in turn, helps the practitioner to choose the most appropriate treatment.

Cynics can be forgiven for pointing out that this new phase may have come about precisely because the old, predictive, astrology was shown to be worthless. An astrology which talks of predispositions rather than future events, and uses the language of depth psychology, cannot be disproved as easily as one which makes precise forecasts. One or two psychologists have taken this line, and have begun to use the art of creative astrology as a weapon in their psychological armamentarium.

The question which keeps coming back at us, however, is the same crude old one: 'Is there anything in it? Is it true?' A few surveys (notably the ones by Michel Gauquelin) indicate that there might be some statistical correlation between a certain type of personality and the birth-dates of the people who exhibit it; or, as Eysenck and Nias write, that 'a baby predisposed to develop a particular type of personality will tend to be born at a moment when one of the planets is at a certain critical position in the sky'. But the results of Gauquelin's survey have been disputed. In any case it might simply have been due to the fact that people who spend the first few months of their lives exposed to the weather conditions of one particular season are more likely to develop into athletic types. The planet Mars need have had nothing to do with it. What is more damning to the astrological case, as Gordon Melton points out,[8] is that the correlations which Gauquelin found between the position of planets at birth and the chosen professions of a large sample of people, though they were statistically significant, bore no relation to traditional astrological correspondences.

Where do these traditional correspondences come from, and how are they justified and explained? The obvious answer is 'from tradition', which is about as circular as describing an archdeacon as a clergyman who performs archidiaconal functions. But it satisfies many New Age astrologers. They see our age as an age which is suffering from a glut of knowledge and a famine of wisdom, and believe that what needs to be recovered is the ancient wisdom of older societies. Those societies lived closer to the unseen world than we do, and that in itself is sufficient reason for taking their insights seriously. We don't ask silly questions of them, like '*How* do you know?' To do so, only exposes our own crassness.

In fact, astrology probably arose in the Babylonian empire of the seventh century BC, from whence it spread westwards. It was Ptolemy in the second century BC who codified it, and it was well known at the beginning of the Christian era (see the reference to the astrologers from the east in Matthew's account of the nativity of Jesus, and the encounter with Simon the Magus in Acts 8.9–13). One way in which its claims were made credible was the doctrine that the soul, leaving its home in heaven for an earthly incarnation, passed through the spheres of the planets and thereby acquired some of their characteristics. The closer the planet to the path of the incarnating soul, the greater its influence on it during its lifetime.

Astrology was suppressed in the Christian world after the time of St Augustine (who died in AD 430), but returned, under the influence of Jewish and Arabian scholars, in the thirteenth century. It reached its zenith at the time of the Reformation, at which time most Christian scholars would have taken its claims seriously, but it declined in the wake of the scientific revival of the seventeenth, and the scepticism of the rationalistic eighteenth, centuries. The Witchcraft Act of 1735 made it possible to prosecute astrologers in the courts, and, for example, W. F. Allen was fined £30 under it after his trial on a charge of fortune-telling in 1917. The repeal of the Witchcraft Act in 1951 has been one factor in the rising tide of astrological activity since then.

Can a Christian be an astrologer? Laurence Cassidy, a Jesuit priest and Professor of Philosophy at St Peter's College, Jersey City, NJ, would answer 'Yes': 'For some six years, [he was writing in 1978] I have taught some astrology here at St Peter's College and no one has ventured to suggest that I am putting my soul in peril by doing so. Of course, most think my mind is becoming enfeebled, but that's another story.'[9] Fr Cassidy sees the claims of astrology as more in the realm of science than of religion, and does not see them threatening the doctrine of human freewill. We do not say that because a person's behaviour is affected by his heredity and his environment, he is therefore deprived of freewill in his actions. No more ought we to do so if we believe there are also astrological influences working upon him. A knowledge of the forces acting upon us can make us more free rather than less; forewarned is forearmed. God is the Creator of the stars and planets. Look at the way in which he taunts Job, who has no more than a human understanding of the ways of the heavens:

Can you bind the cluster of the Pleiades
or loose Orion's belt?
Can you bring out the signs of the Zodiac in their season
or guide Aldebaran and its satellite stars?
Did you proclaim the rules that govern the heavens
or determine the laws of nature on the earth?

(Job 38.31–3)

This is all very well, but we still have to ask the question of whether astrology is successful as a mantic method – and if so, why. The older predictional astrology was discredited by the advance of scientific understanding. The newer astrology is a psychological tool, but if it is successful, is that a placebo effect, due to the skill of the psychologist rather than to the inherent value of the method he uses? We shall see that the same suggestion can be made about the other mantic methods favoured by New Age prognosticators. When they succeed, they may do so because the practitioner is hanging his intuitional (maybe his psychic) skills on the slender hook of a system which gives him a great deal of non-specific information from which he can select the items which seem to him to be most apposite to the client concerned, and which can then be fleshed out from a knowledge of the client's circumstances.

2. The Tarot

The divinatory device which has enjoyed the greatest surge in popularity in recent years is the Tarot. Until the mid-sixties, the only decks available for sale were those created by Aleister Crowley and A. E. Waite, and even these could only be obtained by the cognoscenti from suppliers they knew. Now, new decks appear at the rate of several each year, and guides to the Tarot and its interpretation are on sale in almost every bookshop.

Tarot cards and our present-day playing cards have a common ancestry, but a Tarot deck is more complicated than the playing card one. It contains 78 cards. 22 of them form the 'Major Arcana', and contain representations of archetypal figures such as the Magician, the Hierophant, the Hanged Man, Death, the Lovers, the Sun, and the Fool. The minor cards are in four suits of fourteen cards apiece – the ace, two to ten, page, knight, queen and king of staves or wands, cups, swords, and discs or coins.

The cards are shuffled, laid out in one of a series of possible patterns, and interpreted. Each card has its meaning, though it is a constellation of generalized meanings from which the reader has to select what seems to be most appropriate to the particular 'querent' or client. Thus, as in an astrological reading, the exact information or advice given to the client will not be mechanically read off the spread of the cards, but will depend on the intuitions of the reader. At its most extreme, this leads to the assertion that 'there is no one way of reading the cards which is true or right. Everyone must make out their own interpretation, their own understanding of what each reveals to them ... Be willing to be taught by the Source and not some biased human commentator.'[10]

The pack as now standardized hails from eighteenth-century France, and its symbols and their occult interpretations have links with French and Continental Freemasonry of the period. Their prehistory is a matter of controversy. Many occultists will hold that they originated in the temples and mystery schools of ancient Egypt and were imported into Europe during the Middle Ages. That is now recognized to be a baseless myth,[11] and most historians hold that they are of medieval European origin and were a kind of playing card which became used for occult and divinatory purposes. Tarot images, however, are

> universal and fundamental to the human psyche, instantly recognizable in any guise, however ancient, alien or strange; and there is no doubt that those same images are also symbolic initiatory ones of great antiquity ... Thus it seems logical to assume that the Tarot is a 'modern' initiatory device and also – more importantly – that it actually derives from and incorporates within itself the knowledge and beliefs of *more than one ancient Mystery System.*[12]

Several interpreters of the Tarot[13] link the meanings of its cards with the medieval Jewish mystical and numerological system known as the Qabalah (it is seen as significant, for example, that there are 22 cards in the Major Arcana and 22 letters in the Hebrew alphabet). According to the Qabalah, the universe emanated from the Creator through various levels of existence or *Sephirot* which can be represented on a diagram of the Tree of Life. The *Sephirot* are similar to the various heavens between earth and the abode of God to which Christian writings refer (see, for example, Heb. 4.14; 2 Cor. 12.2). The Qabalistic Tree contains nodal points given the names of concepts such as Wisdom, Mercy, Splendour, Kingdom, etc. It reveals the underlying meaning and structure of the universe by an occult and highly numerological means of interpreting the hidden sense of the Hebrew Scriptures. An edition of Qabalistic texts was published by S. L. MacGregor Mathers ('magician, Rosicrucian, scholar, Freemason, Celtic mystic and co-founder of the Order of the Golden Dawn') in 1887 under the title of *The Qabalah Unveiled*, and reprinted by Arkana in 1991. (The new printing uses the spelling *Kabbalah*.) His widow's Preface to the 1926 edition gives the flavour of the work, in which she writes of Qabalistic knowledge which was never committed to writing but communicated orally from occult teachers. As to its theology, 'the distinction between monotheism, polytheism and pantheism ... hardly exists for the Initiate. Verily there is little difference between a single God and a harmony of Supreme Forces.'[14]

The New Age interpretation of the Tarot symbolism links the meanings of the cards with the archetypes of Jung's psychology: 'In a typical New Age Tarot reading, the cards are not used for "fortune-telling", but as a means for diagnosing the person's current situation in terms of his or her overall spiritual growth.'[15]

The Tarot, like astrology, is therefore attractive to the New Age for a variety of reasons. It claims a great antiquity, and has links with mysteries which have been hidden from all but the favoured few for centuries. These mysteries, it is held, can exert their healing power on people who have been alienated from their true spiritual path by the noisy and bustling technology of modern times. They are easily patient of an interpretation which links them with the psychological theories of C. G. Jung. They do not postulate a personal deity but can work just as well with the concept of an impersonal creative power behind the universe; and they separate earth and heaven by intermediate layers of being.

3. I Ching

Other mantic devices can be described more briefly. Most of them are attractive to New Agers for the same reason as astrology and the Tarot; that is, they claim to come from ancient civilizations which had a greater wisdom than we now possess, but whose knowledge has been handed down to us through the ages, often in secret because their practitioners were persecuted by ignorant modernists or fanatical and dogmatic religionists.

The ancient Chinese method of divination is known as the *I Ching*.[16] Forty-nine stalks of yarrow of differing length are thrown onto the ground and arranged into hexagrams. The patterns are interpreted according to their traditional significance. The pattern of any casting coincides with the quality of the moment at which the stalks were cast and so can reveal itself to the adept. We can also project our own subjective concerns onto an *I Ching* pattern and receive the guidance for which we are asking.

4. Scrying

Other mantic methods are more directly psychic, and depend almost entirely on the sensitive receiving information intuitively. The famed 'crystal ball' is of this nature. The seer looks into it and, in a dissociated or trance state, begins to perceive patterns or figures or images which are the visual representations of information which is received by telepathic or clairvoyant means.

Instead of scrying with a ball, the sensitive can use a reflective surface, such as a bowl of water. Begin

by taking a glass goblet or bowl of spring water and a shiny glass mirror out during a clear night of a waxing moon. When the moon is fairly low on the horizon, newly risen or just setting, catch her light in the water, so that you can see her reflection in it. This moon-blessed water can be used to scry in, placed in a clear vessel on a dark background, perhaps contained within the circle of candle light just as the old witches used to scry in their seething cauldrons. Focus your inner sight on the depths of the water when it has become still, and then relax with your eyes closed. Ask the moon to bless your vision, and gently open your eyes, gazing steadily but without strain into the water. See what you notice, but do it in a calm way, allowing any change to occur without breaking your detached mode of thought. Nothing may happen the first time you try, but if you persist you will begin to see a milkiness in the water, vague patterns of colour, points of light, and over a few sessions, these will grow clearer and eventually become pictures, symbols, numbers, words, figures, or simply voices in your head, telling you things.[17]

5. *Ouija*

There are other ways, akin to scrying, by which the reception of paranormal information may be facilitated. Some sensitives like to handle an object which has been owned by the client, or to which the client has a particular emotional attachment. This is known as 'psychometry'. Others use the ouija board or planchette. This has been used in the reception of channelled information (see Chapter 10 below), though otherwise it is not very prominent in New Age psychism. It is more the sort of thing with which teenagers and the psychologically immature like to experiment. There are dangers in the use of the ouija board and it should not be encouraged.

The board consists of a flat surface with the letters of the alphabet, the numbers zero to nine, and the words 'Yes' and 'No'. A small platform, two or three inches wide, is built on three short legs, smooth-tipped so that they can slide easily. The platform, or 'planchette', has a pointer to show the letters over which it moves to spell messages. The participants maintain fingertip contact with the platform, and it moves around, apparently of its own volition, though actually as a result of unconscious muscular activity on the part of the members of the circle.

The device, according to seasoned psychics, 'has a reputation for attracting the lowest class of entities'.[18] That is, if 'entities' are what it attracts. Other authorities[19] believe that what happens is that a member of the circle unconsciously moves the pointer to spell messages which come from a repressed part of the subconscious and which are unacceptable to the conscious mind, generally because they indicate violence towards oneself or loved ones. The fact that they are suppressed means that the conscious mind cannot cope with them and tries to pass them off (by the psychological mechanism known as 'projection') as coming from some external entity. Their real origin indicates that they are emotionally charged and that the conscious mind has repressed them because it finds them impossible to deal with. Since the board is often used by immature and adolescent characters, there is usually a great deal of psychological sewage around at a ouija session. That, rather than 'low-grade malevolent spirits', is probably why so many people who have experimented with an ouija board have come a cropper.

6. *The human aura*

Mentioned more frequently in New Age circles than such unfashionable things as the ouija board is the human aura. Some people claim to be able to see a glow or aura around a person which enables the sensitive to guess the emotional state or physical health of the client. But, once again, it is not the actual appearance of the aura but the way in which it is interpreted which matters. 'Once you learn to detect the energy field ... you will intuitively be guided to understand the significance of what you can see or sense.'[20]

This phenomenon, so the aura visualizers claim, is what lies behind the way in which saints are shown in Christian art with haloes around their heads. In Lincolnshire until fairly recently there were still a few elderly people to be found who remembered Bishop Edward King (who died in 1910). They would tell you that his face glowed. Not physically, but there was something about him that could only be expressed in that way. Something similar seemed to be happening in the case of one of the leaders of the Welsh religious revival of the early years of this century. Light was observed streaming from the body of Mary Jones, and around the chapel when she was preaching in it.[21] According to Exodus 34.20–35, when Moses had seen the LORD on the holy mountain, the skin of his face shone; and the same happened to Jesus on the Mount of the Transfiguration (Mark 9.2–8).

What is happening? Is there something objective about these accounts? One explanation is that the aura may be seen because some sensitives are adepts at visualization, and therefore project their paranormally-acquired knowledge in visual form. Or it may be that there *is* a quasi-physical aura which some sensitives are able to perceive. There are certainly temperature gradients near the skin of the human body, and quite possibly electro-magnetic gradients as well, and we do not know whether these may not be detectable and therefore visualizable by receptors of sufficient sensitivity such as people who claim to be able to see auras.[22]

Kirlian photography claims to be a scientific way of showing that the aura is objective and capable of being recorded on film. This technique was pioneered by two Russian scientists, Semyon and Valentina Kirlian, and announced in the West in 1970.[23] At the Festival of Mind/Body/Spirit in 1991, visitors were invited to allow one of the stallholders to take Kirlian photographs of their own hands.

In Kirlian photography, an object – a leaf, a human hand, or whatever – is laid on top of the emulsion of a piece of colour film and an electric charge is passed through it. The voltage and frequency are such that a spark could be obtained, but the current is tiny. The interposition of the object prevents the spark and instead, when the film is developed, it appears in silhouette. But it is surrounded by an aura, whose colour and thickness depend on whether the object is living or dead, in good health or otherwise.

The interpretation of Kirlian photographs is disputed. Dr George Blaker, writing on behalf of the Committee for the Study of Scientific Research of the Churches' Fellowship for Psychical and Spiritual Studies, was sceptical. He suggested that the photographs were mere artifacts arising partly from differential conductivity in the layers of the film emulsion, and partly from the effects of moisture on the ionization taking place during the electrical discharge. But the argument still goes on.

7. *Dowsing*

Electromagnetic sensitivity is probably a major factor in dowsing, or divination by the use of a pendulum or forked stick. The stick itself is no more than a device to magnify the tiny twitches of the dowser's muscles as he passes over the ground to be surveyed. If, for example, he holds the stick within a tube so that his hands cannot affect its movement, nothing happens.

Dowsing can be used for any one of a number of purposes. The reputed plans of archaeological sites, including the 'White Church' which was the first building to be erected on the site of Durham Cathedral, have been dowsed by Denis Briggs of Newcastle upon Tyne. His work has been published in a monograph of which Richard Bailey, the Professor of Anglo-Saxon Civilization at Newcastle University, and Eric Cambridge of the Durham University Department of Archaeology, are his co-authors. The success of dowsing over a site is easier to accept than the undoubted fact that some dowsers (Denis Briggs included) seem able to do almost as well on a map or plan as they can perform on the ground. That may indicate that the information which is being projected by the moving pointer has been acquired paranormally rather than geomagnetically. Other dowsers use pendulums to sex day-old chicks or to detect allergies in their patients,[24] and here, too, the results may be due more to paranormal factors than to anything physical or magnetic.

Many of these divinatory methods are amalgams of techniques and sensitivity. The particular method acts as little more than a trigger to allow the gentle art of intuition to take over and grant the diviner access to information which is available (paranormally or otherwise) to the subconscious. Over most mantic activities it is necessary to keep an open and agnostic mind. How far they are genuine human abilities and how far they appear to work because the client is disposed to take an ambiguous message in a more precise sense, we do not yet know. It is the business of scientific parapsychology to examine the claims 'without prejudice or prepossession' (to quote the 1882 prospectus of the Society for Psychical Research). Not all of them are as breathtaking as they are cracked up to be. In many cases, they are clever guesses, inferences from the client's appearance or demeanour, or even the result of the kind of fraud of which stage magicians are such expert practitioners. Dan Korem's book *Powers* gives its readers an insight into how the less reputable psychics can mislead the unwary. Genuine psychic sensitivity is rarer and much less reliable than many 'professional' psychics would have us believe.

What about the reaction of the Christian religion to mantic claims? There are Christians who are wary of them because they belong to the unknown. Certainly, where these methods are necessarily tied to non-Christian religious systems Christians will do well to ask awkward questions about them. And certainly Christians will – and rightly – do their best to discourage people who think to run their lives on the basis of guidance obtained in this kind of way. But maybe these methods show that the human personality has faculties which materialists refuse to examine. If so, those faculties are part of the creation, and it behoves those who worship the Creator God to see that they are used in ways which do him honour. Otherwise, Christians can hardly complain if adherents of other religions and religious systems hijack them and start claiming that one needs to be non-Christian in order to have anything to do with them.

5
Crystal Power

I clutched the tiny pebble of pink quartz in my sticky little palm and awaited developments. It was the start of the workshop on 'Love Crystals and Healing' at the Festival of Mind/Body/Spirit, and I wondered how the presenters were going to be able to help me, 'using crystal energy', to 'release [my]self from the past and experience love in a moment'. The promise also included the invitation to 'find your own healing touch and the miracle of yourself'. It sounded a tall order to achieve in a couple of hours.

In fact, it was simplicity itself. The crystal (most practitioners use rock quartz, either clear or coloured, which is plentifully available) had been prepared beforehand, though we were not told how. All *we* had to do was to prepare ourselves by regaining our own inner unity; then, when we projected our problem into the crystal, it would be solved. The beauty of the crystal, we were told, reflected the beauty of creation, so that love would radiate from it and from us, to touch the whole world. We could test this out by holding the crystal in our hand, touching the fingers of, and looking into the eyes of, the person next to us, and saying, 'I trust you'.

It was too much for the young woman next to me, and she began to sob uncontrollably. Eventually she blurted out that the first anniversary of her father's death was approaching, and I had reminded her of him. Before the workshop had ended, without help from my crystal or hers, I had spoken to her about the work of Cruse–Bereavement Care and the way in which their trained counsellors might be able to help her come to terms with the grief which she had not yet completely worked through. She had realized her mother might need Cruse, but, for herself, thought she might get better help from the New Age festival.

Once more, that line from the hymn flashed through my mind – 'some are sick, and some are sad'. Crystals are much in evidence in New Age shops, and clearly there are people in spiritual or psychological need who believe they can do a great deal for them. What claims are being made?

All kinds of claims. For instance, according to Dr Mike Adams, a Cambridge graduate who holds a Manchester doctorate in zoology and teaches at Bryanston School, 'some form of unknown radiation comes out of domestic electric power sockets and is very powerful ... It is likely that everyone who comes within several feet of power sockets is affected by this invisible energy and is imperceptibly weakened by it.'[1] It may even be a contributory cause of 'a very wide range of disease and illnesses, from fatigue, tension and insomnia to M.S., M.E. and cancers'. But it can be blocked by the use of quartz crystals, which send the radiation back into the socket. A small one can be worn round the neck and a large one placed close to the mains fuse box to prevent the radiation from getting beyond it. After a few weeks of rigorous use, 'the basic internal causes of all illnesses will have disappeared. No new major illnesses should develop from now on', though Dr Adams adds as a precaution against being accused of false claims that 'in spite of that, however, disease symptoms may persist'. Whether they include the symptom of death from an otherwise untreated cancer is not stated.

It is difficult not to be reminded of the eccentric Aunt in James Thurber's *The Night the Bed Fell on Father*, who believed that electricity leaked out of the sockets if the light bulbs were not properly screwed in; but some people, presumably, take Dr Adams seriously. At all events, immediately below his article in *Leading Edge* there is an advertisement from the publishers offering the requisite crystals at £11.95 for the small 'protection pendants' and £14.99 for the kind that can be placed on the fuse box. The technique of creating a previously unfelt need and then showing how one's product can meet it is as crude as that of the evangelist whose stock-in-trade works on 'an exploitative scheme of proclaimed sin, induced guilt, and manipulated release'.[2]

Dr Serena Roney-Dougal would not be impressed by the offer of a crystal in these circumstances. 'If you find a crystal in a special place at a special moment', she writes,

> then this is being given to you by the [Earth-] Mother, and will be a healing tool with which to work and play and enjoy with fond memories of the moment when you found it; but to buy a fancy crystal out of a shop which comes from a quarry or mine from fat commercialists who are only in it for the profit and who are destroying the Mother in the process is abhorrent.[3]

That depends. Is the crystal being used for its physical properties or for its psychic power? Nowadays we all know that crystals, particularly quartz crystals, have many technical uses, though the scientific reasons which enable quartz to be used for those purposes are beyond the comprehension of most of us. But we have heard of quartz watches or silicon chips, so we are inclined to believe what we are told about the potential scientific uses of quartz, particularly if it is couched in the right kind of technical-sounding language. We are also used to reading in the papers every so often that things which we had supposed to be entirely benign in fact pose a hidden health hazard in some way or other which we do not understand but dare not disregard. So we are predisposed to believe it when we read an article about the dangers of something which we had innocently allowed into our homes, particularly if it comes from a person who holds a doctorate in some subject or other.

So, if someone like Dr Adams claims that quartz crystals can neutralize a harmful kind of radiation, we are inclined to believe him. Or if we don't *quite* believe him, we may still play safe and act like the person who bowed his head in reverence every time the Devil was mentioned, on the grounds that 'courtesy costs you nothing, and you never know ...'. The crystal is a form of insurance, and we are not likely to worry where we got it from, so long as it is effective.

But if the crystal is an adjunct to some form of mind-development or soul-culture, then the owner's attitude to it will be crucial. Presumably this applied to the workshop I was describing at the beginning of this chapter. It was certainly true of one other workshop which I attended there, where we were told that we could use crystals in conjunction with soft music and guided imagery to still the critical intellect and enable us to become aware of our own inner powers.

The distinction between the two different kinds of crystal use is not entirely water-tight. All practitioners insist that the crystals need periodic cleansing. Usually this is done by physical means such as immersion in running water; but Dr Adams believes that the simplest method of cleansing a crystal which has become depleted of its store of sub-atomic particles which it needs to 'fight' the power-socket radiation is 'to nestle the crystal in the palm of the hand and hold it against the upper forehead for $\frac{1}{2}$ a minute'.

Some people might suppose that this shows that Dr Adams thinks that the efficacy of the crystal is no more than whatever the user can be persuaded to believe it to be. I would doubt this interpretation. More likely, in a New Age context, the exercise is intended to show that the mind has quasi-physical powers and that the process Dr Adams describes is the method whereby our inherent healing influence can be transferred to the crystal. That would be consistent with other suggestions for cleansing crystals which involve their being 'cleared of all stray and unwanted vibrations' using 'a physical ritual and a strong focussed mind'.[4] This, according to the person who suggested it, is most successful if carried out with a lighted candle and some burning incense whilst the moon is waning.

Here we see, once more, the idea that there is a subtle link between what goes on in the physical and astronomical world and what goes on in the human mind. This is expressed by one writer on crystals (again, using the popular pseudo-scientific terminology which so impresses people who do not have a scientific training) in the following words:

> If you wear a crystal around your neck, that crystal is attuning you to the magnetic core of the Earth, where it came from. It is grounding you. If you take things a step further and begin consciously to attune to the energy of the crystal, you will find a whole new world beginning to open up to you ... You will feel the Earth as a living spirit and learn to sense and work with subtle energies to heal and transform your life ... Once you get hold of a crystal and bond to it, the spirit of the crystal, the crystal energy, starts to work with you on the most subtle levels, to help you balance and develop your own energies.[5]

Once all this has been done, and provided that the crystal is 'respected as an intelligent part of the living spirit of nature',[6] it can be programmed, using concentration, visualization, and will-power, with its specific intention and purpose for use in whatever way its owner wishes. What sorts of intention and purpose? Well, 'some people like to refer to the unique aura or energy of a crystal as the "spirit" of the crystal ... You can project your consciousness inside a crystal and meet and communicate with the spirit of the crystal.'[7] If you lie down and meditate with an amethyst crystal above your head, you can draw its energy into your body. Then you can use it to banish unwanted thoughts or feelings. Or you can programme it to release your guilt and forgive yourself, or enhance your psychic awareness and meet your Inner Guide. It cleanses and balances the psychic aura and can be used for inner healing in conjunction with mantras, chants, incantation, or dance. (All these claims are made by Neil Irwin in his book *Understanding Crystals*.)

It is difficult to see all this as anything more than sheer superstition, or a way by which authors of books, sellers of crystals, or leaders of workshops can batten on the credulity of their clients. Randall Baer, the author of a book entitled *Inside the New Age Nightmare*, came out of that 'nightmare' and is now a 'born-again' Christian. Why did he describe his time in the New Age as a 'nightmare'? We are not surprised to learn that his particular involvement was to have written and lectured on crystal power and that he had two New Age books on the subject to his credit.

The crystal seems to have as much objective power as Linus' security blanket in Charles Schultz's comic strip *Peanuts*. But, like Linus' blanket, it has immense *subjective* power, and therefore needs to be taken seriously. People who use crystals in this way use them because they believe they are under-performing in life, and they think this will help them to develop their potential and release their hidden powers. By the placebo effect, if in no other way, it will work for them (or if it does not, they run the risk of feeling an even more complete failure at running their own lives than they have hitherto imagined themselves to be, and retire disillusioned and unlikely to try *any* kind of psycho-spiritual therapy).

The current craze about crystals is the most immediate and conspicuous sign of New Age interest, but it is the New Age at its lowest level. Crystal-users are pinning their hopes on a power that does not exist. But if all we are thinking of doing about it is to try and persuade the devotees of crystal power of that very obvious fact, we shall be like the people castigated by Jesus for driving a demon out of someone and leaving its place empty. Nature abhors a vacuum, and before you can say 'Beelzebul', seven worse devils will come in, so that the last state of the sufferer will be worse than the first (Matt. 12.43–5). Unless we can give positive hope to the kind of people who need crystals because they cannot otherwise satisfy themselves that they are fulfilling their human potential, we shall simply remove their props and leave them in danger of complete collapse. But that is to anticipate our final chapter, so we will say no more about it for the moment.

6

Green Goddess

Witches have had a bad press for a very long time. Whenever I mentioned that I was looking into witchcraft as part of my study of the New Age, I detected a look of alarm on the face of the person opposite me. I got the impression that I was on a very dubious quest, or (to vary the metaphor) that I was using a much shorter spoon than I ought to have been, and supping with that unmentionable character whom no respectable clergyman ought to be keeping company with.

'Witchcraft' still suggests the sharp-featured old woman over her seething cauldron, with her pointed hat, her wand, and her broomstick, crooning to her black cat or her pet toad, and casting her malevolent spells on all who dared to cross her.

As with that much-maligned monarch King Richard III, it is Shakespeare as much as any single person who is responsible for the inaccurate image. The reason may be the same in both cases. Shakespeare was writing his dramatized version of history for the benefit of the Tudors who wanted to cast their Plantagenet predecessors in as evil a light as possible. So King Richard is portrayed as an implausible hunchback. Similarly, *Macbeth* paints a fantasy picture of the Old Religion to show how powerful and plausible it might seem, but how wicked it really was. Both plays use the same technique – the rewriting of history in the interests of the ruling class, as described so chillingly in George Orwell's *Nineteen Eighty-Four*. The affections of Shakespeare's audiences had to be turned away from old loyalties which might be dangerous to the present powers, whether of Church or state.

The Church certainly had no scruples over the Old Religion or its practitioners, and the witch trials are a shameful blot upon its history. As in more modern times, the trials were often excuses for paying off old scores on people whom the persecutors had imagined had done them some wrong;[1] or (as with the Blood Libel in the case of the medieval Jews or the horrors of Nazi times) they were an attempt to draw people's attention away from the inadequacies of the ruling régime by directing their venom against a scapegoat who could be readily identified and who had not the power to put up any effective opposition. So the lonely old woman with her iron pot and her pet animal, the woman who observed what was going on in the village (and frequently knew more about it than was good for her), the person whose expertise lay in herbal remedies and the ways of the wood, was said to be in league with the Devil and directed by evil spirits. When the new-fangled printing presses began to issue their illustrated broadsheets against those pagan customs which had survived a millennium or more of state Christianity, the horned god of the ancient religion – Herne the Hunter with his stag's antlers – became the image of Satan with his horns and cloven foot.

Persecution rarely exterminates a religion, and the old beliefs simply went underground – for a long time. In 1735, the Witchcraft Act (9 Geo. II, c.5) made prosecutions for 'witchcraft, sorcery, inchantment, or conjuration' void, but only because Parliament was too rationalistic to believe in them. The new Act's purpose was 'for the more effectual preventing and punishing any pretences to such acts and powers ... whereby ignorant persons are frequently deluded and defrauded'. The word 'pretence' in eighteenth-century English meant 'a claim', without necessarily inferring that the claim was invalid (Bonnie Prince Charlie was 'The Young Pretender'), but the context here makes it clear that in the minds of the framers of the legislation, anybody practising witchcraft was *ipso facto* trying to delude her clients.

The 1735 Act was invoked as late as 1944, when Helen Duncan, a noted Spiritualist materialization medium, was charged with 'conspiring to pretend to exercise a kind of conjuration'.[2] Her phenomena were widely believed to have been fraudulently produced, but her offer to exhibit them before the court was disallowed and she was found guilty. Partly as a result of that trial, the 1735 Act was repealed and replaced by the Fraudulent Mediums Act 1951 (14/15 Geo. VI, c.33).

That Act says nothing about witchcraft, though it is still used from time to time in cases involving confidence tricksters who try to relieve unwary clients of large sums of money. It holds no terrors for mere entertainers, who are explicitly excluded from its provisions. Nor can it touch those who genuinely believe in the phenomena they are producing, because it has to be proved that the medium acted for reward, and either used a 'fraudulent device' in the course of what she did, or otherwise acted 'with intent to deceive'. To a lawyer, 'to deceive' means 'to induce a man to believe [anything] contrary to what the person practising the deceit knows *or believes* to be the case',[3] so if she believes in what she is doing, she is clear.

But to return to witchcraft. The repeal of the 1735 Act allowed it into the open, so that gradually, through the swinging sixties of 'everything goes', and on into the New Age nineties, knowledge of, and paraphernalia used by, witches became more and more widely available. Nowadays, books, divinatory cards, boards, and tables, as well as all sorts of tools and regalia, may be readily bought, not only in specialist places like the *Sorcerer's Apprentice* shop in Leeds and various New Age emporia, but also in many a High Street bookshop.

The ideas of witchcraft or, as its practitioners prefer to call it, *Wicca*, are drawing an increasing number of followers. (The words Wicca, witchcraft, wisdom, wise, and wizard, all have a common origin.) According to Marian Green, an author with a number of books on this subject to her credit, 'some seek religious freedom, some wish for magical powers, some wish to re-awaken the ancient links with our Mother Earth, or seek healing of both body and spirit'.[4]

How many there are is hard to tell. Some overestimates put the figure at hundreds of thousands. At the other extreme, Dr Tanya Luhrmann, an anthropologist at that time teaching in Christ's College, Cambridge, wrote in 1989 that she 'would guess perhaps a thousand in England and more in the States'.[5] That is probably to underestimate the matter, since besides those who are formally initiated into covens with a known succession, there are many who practice solitarily, and heaven knows how many who form their own covens or groups without telling any outsiders – what Dr Serena Roney-Dougal calls 'the proliferation of pagan, neo-pagan, wiccan and other grass-roots groups forming spontaneously all over the country'.[6] It is sobering, for example, to ponder the implications of the fact that by the time I bought a copy of Vivianne Crowley's book *Wicca*, the year after its first publication, it was already in its fourth printing.

In addition, there are always the inadequate personalities who seek to bolster themselves up with imagined powers that are secret to themselves but which enable them to fantasize that they are the Clark Kent of the office staff. Others, such as Derry Knight who was convicted in 1986 at Maidstone Crown Court of obtaining over £200,000 by false pretences from a number of Christians who had been convinced that he needed the money to infiltrate an occult organization, are no more than confidence tricksters using ignorance of witchcraft as a lever to extract money from the credulous and unwary. And, even more sadly, there are the wicked or pathological types who use the ideas of witchcraft as a cover for their paedophiliac or pornographic fantasies, or those for whom the idea of witchcraft is simply a part of their diseased psychopathology; their antics are often disproportionately recorded in the popular press. Society will never be entirely rid of such scourges, and whilst we do well to be aware of them, they are not a proper subject for discussion in a book about serious wiccans and their relationship to the New Age. Before we come to the end of this chapter, however, we will need to say something about the public perception of witchcraft and its association with such obscenities.

Within Wicca proper, there are two main kinds of witches; coven wiccans[7] and solitary wiccans:[8]

> Some wish to be part of covens, to share ceremonies and regular meetings with like-minded folk in the comfort of their own homes. Others, however, have heard wilder music, playing to an older beat, and wish to reunite with Mother Nature alone, out of doors, under the light of the stars and changing moonlight in a simpler way.[9]

Both men and women wiccans may properly be called 'witches'. The words 'wizard' and (even more) 'warlock' are disliked within Wicca, and are never used. A small proportion of both solitary and coven wiccans are hereditary followers of the Craft, and may practice it as couples or as whole families. There are also several sub-divisions of each type of Wicca. All of them, however, share certain beliefs, and the picture which follows is necessarily painted with a broad brush, to keep it within reasonable bounds.

Some come to Wicca because they have been revolted by Christian history and practice, and distrust the Church profoundly.[10] An organization, they say, which so persecuted their forebears when it had the authority to do so, ought never to be entrusted with power again. Although the Church is at present powerless to persecute, there are certainly signs from its fundamentalist wing that there are Christians around who would dearly like to reactivate the ancient anti-witchcraft laws if only they could seize once more the reins of power.

Most wiccans, however, regard the Church as no more than an irrelevance and pursue their craft without giving it a thought. Essentially, they wish to align themselves with the forces of nature, with the spirits or 'devas' which lie behind the natural world, and with the Goddess (and, to a lesser extent, the God) whom the natural world represents and embodies. They generally believe that all of nature is sacred and therefore support any Green or ecologically-sound movements. Many of them belong to such organizations as the World Wide Fund for Nature or Friends of the Earth. They do not evangelize or proselytize, and prefer to keep a low profile, though they may be contacted through their many specialized and low-circulation magazines, which may often be seen in the local health or earthcare food shop. Most of them are vegetarian, or even vegan. They believe in the inherent divinity (or potential divinity) of every human being, though they recognize that not everyone has taken steps to realize the divinity within. As the *Song of the Earth* goes:

> I am the Mother Earth, and you're a child to me,
> Discover who you are and seek divinity.[11]

The solitary or do-it-yourself wiccans, those who practice witch-craft on their own and without the support of a coven, are usually people who have romanticized our national pagan past – either pre-Christian or medieval. They wish to recover that pagan past, in an attempt to escape the unnatural life of our over-technologized, twentieth-century cities, with their constant bombardment of the senses by newspapers, advertisement hoardings, sliced bread, sanitized and de-natured food, and the ubiquitous intrusion of the television screen. Christian imperialism, they claim, may have driven the Old Religion underground, but it cannot kill it, for it springs from a harmony between the earth and the people on it which can still be re-established.

So the followers of Wicca seek to rid their minds of all the rowdy clutter which can so easily fill them, and attune to the Goddess, the Earth Mother, 'from whom, ultimately, all knowledge, magic and power flows'.[12] This Goddess is to be found in the things of nature – trees and countryside, streams and sea, moon and moonlight. Similarly, though less importantly for wiccans, there is the God, who is represented either by the sun itself, or by the wild and untamed stag with his proud antlers (a gentle beast, nevertheless, and we should not forget that fact, as it is important in understanding the gentleness of Wicca itself), or by Herne the Hunter, or by the Green Man covered in the leaves of the hedgerow or forest. It is sobering to realize the way in which the ancient Celtic god Cernunnos, the god of the forests often portrayed with antlers growing from his brow, became the 'Green Man' covered in leaves and branches; and how the iconography of the Green Man has been ubiquitous in the art and architecture of a (nominally) Christian civilization for century after century. Anyone wishing for confirmation of this only has to look at the marvellous photographs by Clive Hicks which accompany the text of William Anderson's *Green Man: The Archetype of our Oneness with the Earth.*

The moon and the sun, however, are not themselves the Goddess and God. They only symbolize the feminine and masculine aspects of divinity. Indeed, wiccans are uncertain whether to claim that the Goddess exists in an entirely objective way; she is archetypal, and they believe that, though it is possible to create entities by our belief in them, they may cease to exist if the causative belief dies away. The Goddess is not an external entity which can 'control' worshippers; the worshippers are themselves part of the Goddess – or, to put it in its converse way, the Goddess is part of her worshippers – there is a god (or goddess) within each of us. This is one reason why wiccans are scornful of channelling (a phenomenon which we shall meet in Chapter 10 below). They believe that people should take responsibility for the things they do, not foist them off on some supposed entity which they imagine to be controlling them.

The Goddess is extremely important within Wicca. As a religion, Wicca obviously satisfies those who believe that the feminine element within Christianity has been ineradicably obscured. Many wiccans pity the Christians who have no goddess to worship, and believe that we worship a masculine Trinity[13] and do the best we can with Mary as a substitute Goddess. The Blessed Virgin, so some wiccans believe, acts for us in exactly the opposite way to their Goddess, and serves to repress womankind instead of doing what they recognize as essential, and affirming the feminine within spirituality.[14]

A great deal of powerfully imaginative writing – some of it for children, but with a hidden level which speaks to adults as well – can evoke this sense of the *mysterium tremendum* which wiccans believe lies behind the phenomenal world. We have it in such books as the novels of Charles Williams, or Tolkien's *Lord of the Rings*, or the Narnia chronicles of C. S. Lewis, or *The Wind in the Willows*, or parts of A. A. Milne, or in John Masefield's *Box of Delights*, so imaginatively televised in the late 1980s. That may be why there are some conservative evangelicals who warn against reading such authors (yes, even C. S. Lewis)[15] because they can result in a 'fascination with the occult'. The same sense of the *mysterium tremendum* behind the visible world is endemic in many of the Greek and Latin classics, and in the ancient myths which are tied to the cycles of the seasons. Apuleius' *Golden Ass* is frequently quoted with approval by wiccan authors.

Wiccans invoke the Goddess by magical practice. A sacred circle is created, and cleansed by introducing symbols of the four elements of earth, air, fire and water – for instance, soil, perfume, a lighted candle, and a bowl of water. Within the circle, the invocation takes place. You cannot command the Goddess or 'call her up'; but through meditative techniques, through visualization, through concentration, and often in an altered state of consciousness (whether reverie or trance proper) you can become aware of her, and absorb her divinity and power within yourself. This you can do at any time and for a variety of reasons, but it is especially potent at particular phases of the moon, and it will be linked with the fertility-cycle of the crops. Indeed, the ancient wisdom of the dying and rising vegetation is an archetype of the great Divinity. Jesus himself is included by wiccans among 'the magically born, annually dying and sacrificed hero gods',[16] so they cannot see why there should in theory be any antagonism between Wicca and Christianity, and Marian Green claims to know 'Catholic witches, Quaker, and Church of England witches'.[17]

Besides (or perhaps as manifestations of) the Goddess, there are innumerable sprites and fairies who symbolize or inhabit springs, rivers, trees, clearings or sacred places. They are sometimes known as 'devas', a term much favoured of the type of New Ager who is more into ecology than witchcraft. They have been called the outer forms of our inner archetypes. In themselves they are formless; it is we who give them form – possibly it is even we who give them existence – when we become aware of them and make them visible.[18] Peter Spink, commenting on *devas* from a Christian viewpoint, calls them

> shapes and images [which] rise from the vast storehouse of human folklore carried by the human race from its primitive beginnings. Drawn from the deep subconscious, they belong to an earlier

stage of evolution and are frequently linked to a fear of the elemental forces of nature by which primitive human beings were controlled and dominated.[19]

Accordingly, he warns his readers that 'to concede to these forces god-like qualities is to re-invest them with an authority which they once possessed when human beings were in bondage to them'.[20]

In more modern mythology, they become the 'creatures from Outer Space' who appear from Unidentified Flying Objects.[21] On the other hand, gnomes or small male humanoid creatures may take their origin from memories (passed on through the centuries) of the small dark peoples of Neolithic Britain who were dispossessed by the first Celtic and Iron Age civilization – hence the tradition that they are vanquished by the sight or touch of any metal object.[22]

Once the circle has been created and the methods of invocation by meditation and visualization have been established, the witch can then begin to master the ancient arts and magical crafts. Magic is 'the art of working with change, predicting it and shaping it by our trained wills'.[23] 'Meditation' is not what many Christians have been taught as a method of visualizing and thinking about a biblical incident. Rather, as we saw from the example on pp. 31–2 above, it is entering a state of relaxed absorption and then taking oneself on a kind of 'guided tour' of archetypal imagery, particularly attached to trees, streams, water, and light. If successful, the adept will become aware of, and aligned to, the Goddess and to the cycles of the natural world. The divine Presence is either sensed intuitively or, even, seen to the inner eye as a vision. The deity may then be invoked into the body of the participant, and this leads to an inner transformation. In the words of a contemporary anthropologist who has made a special study of witchcraft, 'the sophisticated theology of modern witchcraft treats these ritual enactments of the agrarian year not only as representations of natural change but of human development and transformation ... Witchcraft is thus explicitly both a religion with intense spiritual experience and a self-consciously transformative and therapeutic system.'[24]

The witch is ready now for all the traditional crafts of the Wise Woman or Cunning Man of the past – whether they be clairvoyance, healing, foretelling, or magic. Healing is often done simply by counselling, because the wiccan will believe that much illness is psychosomatic in nature, although some of it may be a way of repaying karmic debts incurred in a previous incarnation[25] (there can be few wiccans who are not believers in reincarnation). Magic is a way of manipulating the power within us so that it can influence other people or events. That is why Wicca has a high moral code, because power brings responsibility and must be ethically used. The central core of this ethic is expressed in the wiccan saying 'an [i.e. so long as] ye harm none, do as ye will' – remembering that the 'will' is a key concept in Wicca, and means the focused willing, not simply a chance impulse. Wiccans believe that if this teaching is ignored, the harm caused to the other party will rebound threefold on the witch who was the cause of it, either in this world or in her next incarnation.

The other main branch of Wicca is coven witchcraft. In its modern form this has few ancient roots, but derives either from Gerald Gardner in the 1940s or Alex and Maxine Sanders in the 1960s, and hence is termed either 'Gardnerian' or 'Alexandrian' Wicca. Another key figure in coven witchcraft since the late 1970s is Starhawk (Miriam Simos), a San Francisco-based writer, feminist, and political activist, author of *The Spiral Dance*, and *Dreaming the Dark*. Some covens use an eclectic form and draw from both Gardnerian and Alexandrian traditions, and some covens are entirely DIY and draw their practices and their rituals from whatever book the leader of the coven happens to have alighted upon as a guide to the Craft. Again, we must use a broad brush to describe beliefs and practices, and in what follows, the two systems will largely be run together.

Coven witchcraft, though it shares most of the beliefs of individual witchcraft, is – obviously – practised in groups rather than solo. A coven can have up to thirteen members; not all covens are full ones.

Coven witchcraft is more concerned with rituals and ceremonies, dates and seasons, degrees and advancements, than is the solitary form we have so far been describing. It honours the Triple Goddess as maiden, mother and crone – the three aspects of the earth at sowing, harvest, and winter – and the Horned God. There are set rituals, long set speeches, and set forms of dance and chant. It is designed to accelerate personal growth by focusing and training the mind in awareness. It pays particular attention to special festal times such as Imbolc, Beltane, Samhain, and Yule (corresponding with the Christian festivals of Candlemas, May Day, Hallowe'en, and Christmas).

Initiation is by a kind of 'apostolic succession' from an existing coven leader, though (exceptionally) self-initiation is deemed possible.

There are three degrees of initiation. The first effects the spiritual awakening of the initiate and links her to the group mind of Wicca. That is the initiation of birth. Its ritual is redolent of Freemasonry with its cords and its blindfold. Did the founders of modern witchcraft base it on Masonic practices, I wonder? The second initiation is the mystery of death, and the third the mystery of the *Hieros Gamos* or sacred marriage of God(dess) and initiate. Initiations and coven meetings are preferably in the open, as far as the vagaries of the English climate will allow, with the participants 'skyclad' (i.e., unclothed). The third initiation involves sexual intercourse between the initiator and the initiand. This will be carried out 'in token' rather than 'in true' if the persons concerned are not permanently pair-bonded, and in any case, the other coven members withdraw from the vicinity whilst the final phase of the third initiation is carried out.

This whole idea will suggest all sorts of wild fantasies to the prurient imagination, and doubtless there are those who have been attracted to Wicca for this very reason. That is to misunderstand what is going on. The skyclad state exposes the coven members to the direct influence of the forces of earth and air. It also symbolizes their openness and vulnerability to, yet their perfect love and perfect trust of, the rest of the coven. They are unprotected and exposed, fearful yet prepared to go forward. In Wicca it is possible to have nakedness without lasciviousness, because the constraints of normal society are replaced by the religion of the coven. There is no *frisson* of excitement which might lead to impropriety – any more than there is in the naturist camp. (Incidentally, Dolores Ashcroft-Nowicki has written *The Tree of Ecstasy*, a manual of sexual technique in which wiccans married to each other or permanently pair-bonded may delight in each others' bodies and in the sexual act as part of their wiccan pathworkings. Would that a similar manual could be produced by Christians with a Christian understanding of the delights which God our Creator has prepared for us, and in which we could unlearn the negative attitudes born of a distrust of the body which has been hammered home by generations of celibate ascetics who thought their way was the only Christian way of dealing with the body!)

Witchcraft, then, is an intuitive rather than a logical religion. If the last few pages have made it sound like a cult of unreason, we may need to be reminded that there are arguments in favour of taking it seriously, though they are based on parapsychology rather than conventional science. They are rehearsed in her book *Where Science and Magic Meet* by Serena Roney-Dougal, one of the few people in England today with a doctorate earned by research in parapsychology.

She reminds us that today's physicists know from Heisenberg's 'Uncertainty Principle' that the observer and the system observed are not inseparable. What happens in the universe is affected by the observer. Within the human brain, mind exerts its power over matter at the synapses where the process of thought causes neurones to fire, and tiny electrochemical and other stimuli cause changes which result eventually in macroscopic changes to the world outside. If it is possible to affect other people's minds telepathically and the outside world by what the parapsychologists call psycho-kinesis, then there is every reason to believe that thoughts in the mind of a witch can cause the effects which she believes they do. We should not lightly underestimate the power of a focused will.

Dr Roney-Dougal wonders whether the site of this activity might not be in the brain's pineal gland. This gland secretes hormones which put us into that kind of mood which is known to be especially conducive to success in experiments in telepathy. It is also sensitive to changes in the earth's magnetic field. It has been shown that cases of psychic communication are more frequent when the geomagnetic field is quiet, and also that Unidentified Flying Objects are more frequently reported at times of geomagnetic stress which can cause hallucinogens to be secreted by the pineal gland. Stone circles, holy places, and ley-lines are all associated with microscopic anomalies in the earth's magnetic field. It will be interesting to see whether Dr Roney-Dougal's hypothesis stands up to the testing it is sure to be receiving over the next few years.

So what ought we to think about modern witchcraft? Its purpose is to bring about an inner transformation. This is something which is more a matter of intuition and feeling than of logic or thinking. It involves the right hemisphere of the brain and the emotional centres in the mid-brain which have been bypassed in too much of our present-day Western civilization.

But, although it is clear 'that its combination of spiritual immediacy, powerful nature imagery and magical practice speaks to many people, and that their experience of the practice is positive and rewarding',[26] there are *gravamina* which can be laid at the wiccan door. However haunting its language (and when well done, it can easily invoke the numinous in its readers), witchcraft even at its best is a return to a primitive religion which modern understandings of the world have increasingly discredited over the last few centuries.

It certainly cannot easily coexist with many central Christian ideas. The 'Goddess' for wiccans is a different concept from 'God' as conceived by Christians. For example, the important person is the witch herself. The Goddess waits to be invoked, but will never force herself upon anyone, and once she has been invoked, it is the inherent divinity of the witch herself (or her share in the divinity of the Goddess) which enables things to happen.

Most of what 'happens' is in the self-awareness of the witch, and this seems to be primary. Wiccans will claim that the existence of even *one* perfectly-centred person will have its effect on the total surroundings of that person, and that the good which is done to the earth by the existence of Wicca is incalculable; but all the same, it certainly seems to the outsider that what is primary is the self-realization of the practitioner, and that the helping of others, or the healing of the earth, takes second place. This makes it hard to rebut the charge that Wicca is a sophisticated system of self-centred soul-culture. It is certainly different in many ways from the ideas of Christian prayer.

The understanding of evil is ambivalent. In the books about the Craft, there is very little mention of the possibility of evil; but witches themselves are acutely conscious of the dangers they face from wicked sprites and other kinds of ill-wishing entities which crowd around them and need to be banished by the cleansing of the circle before the ceremonies of the Craft may safely be begun. In all this, however, evil seems to be treated as something external to the practitioner (unless there· has been the unhappy experience of possession), and the assumption throughout the manuals of instruction is that the will and personality of the one who desires initiation is pure, and free from undesirable conscious or unconscious hidden motives.

Wiccans are individualists. They do not try either to evangelize or proselytize. The Craft grows, not by evangelism, but because people enquire about it and want to discover what it is all about. Though, as we have seen, wiccans believe that a positive, centred, morally conscious individual exerts a great influence for good all around, they do not organize themselves in any political manner in the way that the Christian churches, for example, try to lobby Parliament when legislation is under consideration. Perhaps this is because they have for so long been not only a tiny minority but a persecuted minority.

Can Christians pretend to any superiority in this respect? After all, until the time of Constantine and the adoption of Christianity as the official religion of the Roman Empire, the same was true of them. There is, in any case, something to be said for the view (not confined to wiccans) that any religion in power is, *ipso facto*, a debased and a dangerous religion. Once any religion gets power, it is more likely to suppress than to try to refute those with whom it disagrees. Perhaps that is why heresies which Christians thought were past their sell-by date, keep on reappearing![27]

At all events, we should acknowledge that the longstanding continuance and current resurgence of witchcraft witness to truths about the earth and our relationship to it which Christians need to incorporate within their understanding and daily practice of the Faith if it is to appeal at all to those who prefer the blandishments of what Vivianne Crowley calls 'The Old Religion in the New Age'.

Unfortunately, we cannot leave the subject without some reference to allegations of Satanism and even of child abuse which have recently been levelled against witchcraft.

Witches do not worship Satan. That was a libel foisted upon them by Christians who believed that any non-Christian religion was of the Devil, and who began to portray Satan in the guise of Herne the Hunter or of the horned god of wiccan lore. Some witches may honour Lucifer – but Lucifer is not the creature whom the Christians think of as the first of the fallen angels, who by his fall became transformed into the abomination of all desolations ('How art thou fallen from heaven, O Lucifer, son of the morning!' [Isa. 14.12 in the King James version]). For wiccans, he is, quite simply, the Bringer of Light and has no sinister connotations at all. He is another of the manifestations of divinity immanent in creation. That is why, in another area of New Age thinking, the publishers of Alice Bailey's works used to be called the Lucifer Trust. In the end the misunderstandings were so severe that it was renamed Lucis.

Wiccans are not Satanists. Satanists are people who have so reacted against Christianity that they wish to worship Christianity's archetypal enemy. They are generally sick people, particularly if they claim to be followers of witchcraft and commit abominations in its name in order either to excuse their pornographic excesses or feed their psychotic delusions or blackmail their victims or frighten those whom they want to get into their clutches.

What wiccans do is not at all like what children do at Hallowe'en, and to try to stop the folk-practices nowadays associated with 31 October (as some evangelicals do) on the grounds that they may lead to an 'unhealthy obsession with the occult' seems to me to be going over the top.[28] Hallowe'en for most children means fun, parties, and dressing up for 'trick or treat'. For small children, it is far more to do with coming to terms with fear of the unknown or fear of the dark – either the external dark or the dark side of themselves – than with becoming enslaved to 'the occult'. It may be a way of learning about folk-traditions and the pre-Christian beliefs of the people of these islands, but it is not a way of introducing them to things that Christians ought not to know anything about. Witches themselves ought to be more concerned about the mis-picturing of themselves and their beliefs by children in their Hallowe'en revels than Christians are about the evening's activities acting as propaganda for the Old Religion. The fact that the witches are not greatly bothered about it, ought probably to indicate that neither should the Christians be.

Wiccans (except for the few hereditary witches) do not involve children in their practices. Accusations of 'Satanic child-abuse' are one of the reasons for the existence of ORCRO – 'The Occult Response to the Christian Response to the Occult'.[29] ORCRO's bitter publications, which are a counterblast to what they call the 'fundies' (i.e. fundamentalists), are a sorry sample of what happens when the pot and the kettle get involved in mutual mud-slinging. (Incidentally, many wiccans have never heard of ORCRO.)

A recent issue of *Fortean Times*[30] examines the child-abuse allegations in some detail and concludes that the affair is very similar to classical witch-hunts, fed by ignorance, misinformation, and fear. The European medieval witch-hunt throve upon the fantasy of 'a baby-killing, cannibalistic, incestuous, orgiastic Devil-worshipping community'. But then, the persecutions of Christians in the early years of our era fed upon similar misinformation. Their opponents circulated allegations that the Christians had a revolting rite of initiation in which they drowned babies, and that in their meetings, after eating the flesh and drinking the blood of a dead man, they went on to engage in what they called love-feasts where the wine flowed freely amongst the men – and women – who were present (nudge, nudge; wink, wink).

Wicca does not involve Satanism, and it does not involve child-abuse. If we are to engage as Christians with witchcraft, let us engage with it as it really is, not with a fantasy largely of our own making.

7
Caring for Creation

We were seated on a small ring of chairs in the basement hall of a central London church (no prizes for guessing which one). In the middle, on a circular rug, there stood a posy of flowers, a quartz crystal, a New Zealand paua shell, a few pine cones, one or two hand-made ceramic bowls, and a lighted candle. The group was called Creation-Centred Spirituality.

That particular evening's subject was 'deep ecumenism'. The kind of ideas which were expressed in the presentation and the discussion which followed were that if we are to live in harmony with the earth, we have to go behind the sophisticated modernity of so much of our present-day religious thought and practice. An acid test to apply to any religion is to ask of it the question, 'Is it happy with the primitive?' The ancient wisdom (whether Hebrew or Celtic) was acutely aware of the interface between the visible world and that which lies, unseen, behind it. It is a wisdom we can all discover.

If we do so, we will find that it leads to a relaxed delight, where we accept people for what they are and do not try to mould them to our own patterns. We should emulate the delighted play which the Creator God had with Wisdom before the world came into being. There is a marvellously evocative passage in the Book of Proverbs in which Wisdom says she was created by the LORD 'before all else that he made ... in earliest times, at the beginning, before earth itself' and that she 'was at his side each day, his darling and delight, playing in his presence continually' (Proverbs 8.22–3, 30).

The ecumenism that we need if we are to love the created world aright is an ecumenism that transcends the differences between faiths. It is only frightened people who put up barriers. Our business is to release the captives, not hem them in within systems of philosophy or religion.

My experience that evening was far from unusual. In the previous chapter, we concentrated on one particular kind of nature-religion which is having a renaissance in a New Age context, but wiccans are not the only ones to wish that the Earth was better honoured. They are joined in this by people of other religions and of none. Christians, too, are becoming increasingly aware of their duty to the environment, and increasingly embarrassed and penitent about the shameful way in which former generations treated the material creation, and how they thought about it.

For that old attitude, Christianity has to take a large share of the blame. To quote two examples only, both lifted from Ian Bradley's book *God is Green*:[1] Cardinal Newman's article on 'Animals' in the *Catholic Encyclopaedia* included the comment that 'we may use them, we may destroy them at our pleasure . . . for our own ends, for our own benefit or satisfaction'. And John Dickie, Moderator of the General Assembly of the Church of Scotland, wrote in 1930 that 'the world exists for our sakes and not for its own'. We shall come to the roots of this attitude later. For the moment, let us simply note that it is an attitude which many present-day Christians would find deeply repulsive. It has certainly repelled the wiccans, who believe that Christians 'worship the sky father (Our Father who art in heaven), the sun god born at the winter solstice, and deny any homage to the mother, to the earth'.[2]

Many Christians see the need to work with all people of good will, whatever their religious beliefs, if we are to restore harmony between humankind and the earth which sustains it. This attitude came to the fore in the late 1980s in a series of inter-faith Creation-centred liturgies which were staged in cathedrals and major churches. Christians of a theologically conservative disposition were alarmed and felt that the integrity of their faith was being compromised by being put on an apparently equal footing with incompatible beliefs. The less theologically sophisticated probably thought the Churches should have declared themselves in favour of environmental conservation long ago, and were at last catching up on the concerns of the rest of humanity.

With all this as background, it is not surprising that there is a strong Green strand within New Age thinking. The Green movement 'is the physical aspect of the neo-pagan spiritual movement to honour and love and cherish and care for the Earth'.[3] We saw this in the last chapter, in the pagan and wiccan revival, but it is obvious elsewhere. Wherever Green activists are around, New Agers are not far behind. Healthfood and earthcare shops frequently act as meeting-points or information centres for New Age concerns. Many New Agers are vegetarians or vegans.

The north-east of Scotland is the site of one of the most significant focal places in New Age ecological awareness. The story of what has been happening there has been told by Carol Riddell in *The Findhorn Community: Creating a Human Identity for the 21st Century*.[4] In the early 1960s, three friends, Peter and Eileen Caddy and Dorothy Maclean, were working on a gardening project at Findhorn Bay on the Moray Firth. Dorothy believed she was in touch (by channelling, about which see Chapter 10 below) with fairy beings or nature spirits which were associated with particular plant species or with the environment generally. These angelic archetypal forces were called *devas* (the Hindi word for a god). Some devas are specific to a species (the pea deva was the first to be contacted); others, like the landscape deva, relate more generally. The ancient god Pan and his elemental kingdom were close at hand. Dorothy Maclean was told that the garden would succeed if they co-operated with the devas, sought their advice, and gained their permission to work the site. Sure enough, the garden prospered amazingly, and raised crops the like of which had never been seen before in that part of the world.

David Spangler, whose writings have been particularly influential within this aspect of New Age thought, joined the small group in the early 1970s, and it continued to expand. In 1971 the Findhorn Trust was created. The Findhorn Foundation followed in 1972. By 1989 there were 153 members of the community, from seventeen different countries (though none from the Third World or the Eastern bloc), a prospering trading centre, publications, and an educational programme on spiritual and holistic lines which attracts short-term visitors in considerable numbers.

The Community aims to live in oneness with every living thing, so that it can send out love and healing through a deep sense of the sacred in the things of everyday. Its publications include a calendar with breathtakingly beautiful Nature photographs captioned with messages from the devas. The message for July 1991, for instance, from the Lilium Auratum deva, tells us that

> It is high time for humans to branch out and include in your horizon the different forms of life which are part of your world. You have been forcing your own creations and vibrations on the world without considering that all things are part of the whole, as you are – placed there by divine plan and purpose. Each plant, each mineral, has its own contribution to make to the whole, as has each soul. Humans should no longer consider us as unintelligent forms of life to be ignored.

There is little in that quotation that Christians would want to take issue with, except taking too seriously the alleged source of the teaching. As Canon Peter Spink has written about the devas: 'It is often not realised by those who carry out incursions into the lower kingdoms, that to invest these forces with god-like powers carries with it the very real danger of re-investing them with an authority which they once held when man was in bondage to them.'[5] He quotes St Paul, in Colossians 2.8: 'Be on your guard. Do not let your minds be captured by delusive speculations centred on the elemental spirits of the world and not on Christ.'

The New Age does not, however, stop at rediscovering the elemental spirits within the natural world. It sees the Earth herself as divine, as Goddess. It was James Lovelock, a distinguished scientist, and FRS since 1974, who first suggested

the hypothesis that the entire range of living matter on Earth, from whales to viruses, and from oaks to algae, could be regarded as constituting a single living entity, capable of manipulating the Earth's atmosphere to suit its overall needs and endowed with faculties and powers far beyond those of its constituent parts.[6]

His neighbour, William Golding, the Nobel laureate in literature, suggested 'that this creature be called Gaia, after the Greek Earth goddess'.[7] Country people, says Lovelock, see the idea of Gaia as so obvious and true that they wonder why anybody should be either excited, or even surprised, at its rediscovery.

Gaia is an idea which appeals to the poetic and visionary in our makeup. It has been beautifully expressed by Elisabeth Sahtouris, the co-director of the International Institute for the Environment:

We now recognise the Earth as a simple self-creating being that came alive in its whirling dance through space, its crust transforming itself into mountains and valleys, the hot moisture pouring from its body to form seas . . . The tale of Gaia's dance is thus being retold as we piece together the scientific details of our planet's dance of life. And in its context, the evolution of our own species takes on a new meaning in relation to the whole.[8]

Once we have given the earth the *name* of a divinity, it is but a short step to divinizing it and all that is in it. In this way New Agers emphasize the honour they pay to the earth and objectivize the care they have for it.

As a symbol of this, they take the rainbow. Within New Age iconography, the multi-coloured semicircle is ubiquitous. It appears, like a trade-mark, on notepaper, on tea-towels, on shop-fronts, in advertising, on publications. A New Age ecology-conscious quarterly, founded in 1991, is called *The Rainbow Ark*.[9]

In the Judaeo-Christian scheme, the rainbow in the sky symbolized the love of God for his creation and the covenant he made with Noah and his descendants that never again would disaster overwhelm the earth (Genesis 9.12–17). Thus we could be bidden (Ecclesiasticus 43.11) to 'look at the rainbow *and praise its Maker*'. But if we do away with the idea of the Creator God, and think of the creation as self-made and self-sustaining, there is nothing left to praise but Gaia herself, and the rainbow becomes her symbol rather than the symbol of her Creator. Indeed, 'creation' is hardly a proper word to use. If there is no Creator and things have not been created, how can we talk of the 'creation'? Things simply *are*.

Instead of God being *in* all that is, so that he can reveal himself anywhere and be found anywhere, we have the idea that God *is* all that is, and the being of God (or Goddess) is limited to the creation. That creation may include things invisible, like the devas, as well as the visible universe, but there is nothing behind and beyond it.

The first idea (God is in everything, but his being is greater than everything) is known as panentheism and is consistent with a Christian theology. The second idea (God is everything that is, and the totality of the creation is a sufficient description of him or her) is pantheism, a philosophy against which Christian theologians have consistently set their faces. That little syllable '-en-' contains a vital distinction. In pantheism, divinity is entirely immanent within the created order. Panentheism allows for that subtle blend of immanent and transcendent in God which is one of the glories of the Christian revelation.

This means that it is essential for Christians, if they are to engage with the spirit of the New Age, to define their attitude to, and their doctrine of, creation.

Those New Agers who have rejected Christianity because of its lack of reverence for the material creation may have been mistaken. It is at least possible that, in this respect, the barriers between them and the Christians are a good deal less impermeable than they imagined. What New Agers aver (and Christians should join them in this) is that there is 'an essential link between the human race, all sentient beings and the planet itself. The interdependence of life is now beyond question. The recognition of this ranges from the ecologically concerned to the mystically aware. Indeed these two frequently appear as complementary aspects or facets of a single perception.'[10]

So, these bodies of ours are made of the same stuff as the rest of the earth, and what happens to them materially is of immense significance to us. An asceticism which devalues the body and its physical or sexual enjoyment, on the grounds that they are earthy and not spiritual, is unworthy of a theology which gives the material world its proper importance. On the other hand, discipline is not the same as asceticism, so that New Agers – and many Christians – will use (for example) the physical exercises of yoga or kundalini in order to awaken the spiritual by a disciplined use of the material. We should enjoy the earth and affirm the body; they are good. How many Christians see bodily enjoyment as a source of real or potential guilt? And how wrong they are in so doing! But how few sermons make this kind of point?

But that is not the whole story. Besides this, we are capable of transcendence. Christians believe that we have a destiny which lies beyond the earth. There is no need to fall back on a doctrine of reincarnation, as if we are incapable of realizing our potential except by returning time and again to this planet. We are *more than* creatures of the earth. Similarly, there is no reason why Christians should not see the earth herself as *more than* the physical, material, visible, tangible, thing which is obvious to our five senses.

Those who call earth 'Gaia' are trying to disabuse us of the materialistic doctrine that there is nothing spiritual about the material. Christians should rejoice that they have allies, even though they will then need to point out that agreement between themselves and their allies is less than one hundred per cent. It was not a Christian who wrote that

> quite possibly the blackest magicians of our time are those scientists and intellectuals who deny that there is 'godness' in the world [and] ... those psychologists who were so mindless that they tried to say we were 'stimulus-response' machines feeling and thinking nothing – without a soul, without a spirit ... This is black magic and it has created a materialist age that is literally murdering the planet.[11]

Anyone who can write like that, even though she is scathing about the effects on the earth of the influence of Christianity, should be seen as a potential ally rather than an enemy. After all, our faith, too, affirms the earthly grounding of the human race. To it we add our heavenly potential. We do not need to deny the one in order to affirm the other.

So, Christians will agree with those who say that the body is a machine for manipulating the matter in the physical world, or that it is a material vehicle for consciousness. But they will also, and more fundamentally, agree with those who say it is more. In Christian terms, it is the temple of God's Holy Spirit. Our understanding of the transcendence of God will not allow us to go along with those New Agers who say that we are all divine, although we will want to say that we are *capax divinitatis*. Nor will we want to say that the Earth is divine, although the divinity of the Creator God can be discerned within his creation.

Let us, then, try to see what a theology which combines a reverence for creation with a Christ-centred view of the world, can look like. Who knows, we may even surprise ourselves!

A significant name in this connection is that of Matthew Fox. He is a Roman Catholic Dominican priest who founded, and directs, the Institute in Culture and Creation Spirituality in California. In the late 1980s he was in trouble with Vatican authorities for his writings, but the experience seems to have left him unabashed and he has recently followed up his book *Original Blessing* with a further one entitled *Creation Spirituality*. He is a frequent lecturer both in Britain and America, and his allies include the wiccan Starhawk, whom he quotes frequently and with approbation. It is his conviction that at least since the time of St Augustine (AD 354–430), Christianity has gone astray through its over-emphasis on a theology of sin, fall, and redemption.

Instead of harping on original *sin*, he believes that we should be celebrating the original *blessing* of being part of God's good creation. The fall/redemption theology keeps the poor poor and minorities in their place. It is a theology of the oppressor.[12] It is in danger of forgetting that God made this earth, including the people within it, with their various cultures and sexual orientations. The Creator God delights in his creation, and we should preach a religion of world-affirmation, not the false gospel of the fear of a wrathful God. If we call ourselves miserable worms, we are doing ourselves no good and insulting the worms. The primitive religions are creation-centred and world-affirming, and have much to teach us.

Matthew Fox (like John Hick in *Evil and the God of Love*) thinks we would do well to abandon St Augustine and adopt the earlier theology of St Irenaeus. Irenaeus was a second-century Christian writer who taught that evil came about because of the imperfections of a world in the making rather than because of the fall of an originally perfect cosmos.

Admittedly, even Creation Spirituality needs to watch its step. It needs criticism and direction. Not everything that we *can* do is good for ourselves and the earth. 'Our creative energy needs some steering and some directions to follow if it is to save and liberate and not enslave and destroy.'[13] Power corrupts, as it has corrupted the Church ever since Christianity became a state religion in the time of Constantine in the fourth century. So we should 'pray that creation spirituality will always be a minority and remnant church',[14] lest success takes the blessing away from it.

Like all would-be reformers, Matthew Fox has come in for a good deal of criticism.[15] One writer complains that he is creation-confined rather than creation-centred, 'shallow concerning evil, malnourished in his Christology',[16] ignorant of the relationship between asceticism and love of the creation, and heretical in his rejection of the God of the Old Testament. That overstates the case. It is more likely that Fox is right in what he affirms whilst being wrong in what he denies. A creation-centred theology does not have to be argued in *opposition* to a fall/redemption theology. Both can be true. Indeed, a fall/ redemption theology *needs* a prior creation from which to fall. It is true that we should affirm the goodness of God's creation; but when we do this, we soon find ourselves coming up against the fact that the creation and the creatures in it are not as wholly good as God intended them to be. What *is* wrong, and Fox has done well to pull us up short and realize it, is to *begin* with sin rather than with creation.

Unfortunately, even our liturgies get things the wrong way round (and, if *lex orandi* is *lex credendi*, this is not surprising). Morning and Evening Prayer in the 1662 Anglican Prayer Book, the preferred option within Rite A service of Holy Communion in the Alternative Service Book 1980, and the current Roman Catholic rite, all bid the worshippers confess their sins before they get on to anything more exciting. Maybe this is logical, but psychologically it is disastrous. The 1662 Holy Communion, and ASB Rite B, get it far better. In those liturgies, we first let the sheer goodness and numinous awe of God seep through into our consciousness. Only at a much later stage in our act of worship do we so realize our shortcomings that we feel we must halt the progress of the liturgy and confess our sins. When that has been done, we can resume the movement towards taking God's nature within ourselves in the sacramental action.

So far, we have been thinking about ourselves as human creatures, and our relation to God. We are, however, but one part of creation. How should we most properly think of the rest – of that more than ninety-nine point nine nine nine per cent of what God has made? And have we not been intolerably self-centred in the first place, in thinking of the human part of creation as automatically deserving Most Favoured Nation status? New Agers realize that we cannot solve our ecological problems without rethinking the whole of our spiritual relation to the Earth. Christians need to do the same, but they will want to approach it by asking wider and broader questions about *God's* relation to what he has created.

We start off at a disadvantage. As we have already seen, that verse (Genesis 1.28) about humanity having dominion over the earth has had the direst of results in the way in which we have felt justified in treating the material creation. 'Be fruitful, and multiply, and replenish the earth, and subdue it: and have dominion over the fish of the sea, and over the fowl of the air, and over every living thing', it went, in the King James Version so familiar to our forebears. We heard the word 'subdue' and forgot the word 'replenish', and we heard the word 'dominion' and forgot that the ruler who had dominion over his subjects also had responsibilities towards them. That allowed us to take and take and never give back; to squander the fossil remains of forests which had taken a million years to build up, and burn them in a generation; to make dustbowls out of wheatfields and deserts out of fruitful ground; and to believe that, as lords of creation, we were not only allowed but divinely commanded to do so.

Even when we thought we were being sensitive towards nature, we were seeing her simply as there in order to provide nourishment – or poetic inspiration, or sermon illustrations – for ourselves. What anthropocentric arrogance!

For instance, are we singing a hymn in praise of nature when we put 'There is a book, who runs may read' on the Sunday list? No. John Keble wrote it (1819), not to praise nature, but to show how nature could teach theological lessons to us:

> The glorious sky, embracing all,
> Is like the Maker's love . . .

or

> The dew of heaven is like thy grace,
> It steals in silence down;

and so on. Nature, here, is no more than a quarry for holy similes.

St Francis' *Canticle of the Sun* is often held up as an example of the way in which Christianity affirms the natural world. Most people, however, know it only in the metrical version of W. H. Draper (1855–1933), 'All creatures of our God and King'. As Francis originally wrote it, it celebrated nature from a very anthropocentric viewpoint; the creatures were *our* brothers and sisters, and (for instance) water glorified God by being serviceable to man.

Even the marvellous nature-mysticism of Thomas Traherne (*circa* 1670), for all its lyrical beauty, is man-centred and sees nature as being there for our sakes. Traherne knew how to look on nature with the amazed freshness of a child, whose eye had not been sated by frippery delights, and to whom 'all appeared new, and strange at first, inexpressibly rare and delightful and beautiful'.[17] He remembered his childhood as the son of a Hereford cobbler, and the way he wandered to the gates of the city and saw, with wondering eyes, the fields beyond:

> the green trees when I saw them first through one of the gates transported and ravished me, their sweetness and unusual beauty made my heart to leap, and almost mad with ecstasy, they were such strange and wonderful things ... The corn was orient and immortal wheat, which never should be reaped, nor was ever sown. I thought it had stood from everlasting to everlasting.[18]

But it was still all there for man, not in its own right:

> God hath made it infinitely easy to enjoy, by making everything ours, and us able so easily to prize them ... The Earth itself is better than gold, because it produceth fruits and flowers ... You never enjoy the world aright, till the sea itself floweth in your veins, till you are clothed with the heavens, and crowned with the stars: and perceive yourself to be the sole heir of the whole world.[19]

Nature is there for human consumption, its prodigality there simply for *us* to enjoy. Like the author of Gray's *Elegy*, we are made to feel that it would all be wasted if we were not there to appreciate it:

> Full many a flower is born to blush unseen,
> And waste its sweetness on the desert air.

Is that right? Is sweetness and beauty unseen, a waste? There is a strong strand within the Old Testament which sees nature as something which praises God in its own right, and not simply as something which has been put there to serve humans. It comes out particularly in some of the Psalms:

> The heavens declare the glory of God:
> and the firmament sheweth his handywork.

> Thou deckest thyself with light as it were with a garment:
> and spreadest out the heavens like a curtain.

> The lions roaring after their prey:
> do seek their meat from God.

> Fire and hail, snow and vapours:
> Wind and storm, fulfilling his word.

> The little hills shall rejoice on every side.
> The folds shall be full of sheep:
> the valleys also shall stand so thick with corn,
> that they shall laugh and sing.[20]

Then there is the *Benedicite*, from the Apocryphal writings and included within Anglican Morning Prayer: 'O all ye works of the Lord, bless ye the Lord.' It is a paean of praise to God, offered in the name of the whole gamut of creation, starting with the angelic realms, moving on via the skies and earth and seas, and ending with the children of men praising him and magnifying him for ever.

This Old Testament expression of joy at the way in which the natural world exists because God has made it, and praises God by being itself, may have been muted in Christian thought, but it has never been entirely lost. It comes across, almost perfectly, in W. H. Draper's paraphrase of St Francis' *Canticle of the Sun*, which we have already mentioned:

> Thou burning sun with golden beam,
> Thou silver moon with softer gleam,

> O praise him, O praise him,
> Alleluia!

Two further examples, both from the eighteenth century, must suffice. The first is that familiar hymn by Joseph Addison,

> The spacious firmament on high,
> With all the blue ethereal sky,
> And spangled heavens, a shining frame,
> Their great Original proclaim.[21]

The second is in that remarkable prose poem by the eighteenth-century writer Christopher Smart, which Benjamin Britten set to music as a verse anthem:

> For I will consider my cat Jeoffry.
> For he is the servant of the Living God, duly and daily
>   serving him.
> For at the first glance of the glory of God in the East he
>   worships in his way.
> For this is done by wreathing his body seven times round
>   with elegant quickness.
> For he knows that God is his Saviour.
> For God has blessed him in the variety of his movements.
> For there is nothing sweeter than his peace when at rest.

Christopher Smart may have been adjudged insane, but he has a deal to teach the sanity of the rest of us.

If we will not learn this lesson from our Judaeo-Christian heritage, let us learn it (as New Agers know how) from elsewhere. The Druid tradition in Britain and Europe believes it is in touch with our pagan roots, and keeps many of the same festivals as does Wicca. Philip Carr-Gomm's *The Elements of the Druid Tradition* explains their beliefs and practices, and the way in which they honour the spirits of the earthly creation.

But closer to New Age hearts is the North American indigenous culture, which understands the material creation better than we deracinated Westerners will ever do. Steven Charleston, Bishop of Alaska, himself a Choctaw Indian, points out that 'America's tribal people . . . shared [with ancient Israel] a deeply theological understanding of the intimate relation between people, land, and nationhood

... The connection between American Indian tribes and the land is intensely spiritual ... This parallel with the redemptive history of Israel is so close as to be almost theologically intertwined.'[22]

Bishop Charleston goes on to suggest that for Americans, their native culture can be a real Old Testament, leading to a better Christian understanding of the relationships between God, human-kind, and nature:

> The exploration into the theological tradition of Native America is a journey toward discovery ... It is a pilgrimage. It is a walk in faith to trace the path of God through America, to see where God has been and what God has done; to listen to the testimony of those who have seen God passing among them and to hear their witness to the truth of God's love in history.[23]

After so moving a testimony, it is hardly necessary to quote the well-known words of Chief Seattle.[24] But I will do so, because it underscores the way in which a true spirituality – whether Christian or not – respects the material environment as part of the mystery of God's creation (a mystery of which we human beings are a part). In 1854, the white men wished to purchase a huge tract of native land and create in return a 'reservation'. Chief Seattle replied:

> How can you buy or sell the sky, the warmth of the land? The idea is strange to us. If we do not own the freshness of the air and the sparkle of the water, how can you buy them? Every part of this earth is sacred to my people. This earth is precious to [God], and to harm the earth is to heap contempt on its creator.

What can we say but 'Amen'? If only we Christians could follow Chief Seattle! If only we could realize that our duty to the Creator of the earth and of ourselves includes the call for a deep respect for the things he has made, there would be no need to divinize the earth herself. We could even (if we wished) recognize the devas or spirits of nature – not as divinities in their own right, but as beings who owe their existence to God almighty, maker of all things, visible and invisible. They could be seen as part of the great chain of being which Christian tradition has acknowledged as originating from God and including hierarchies of angelic beings as well as the tangible creatures of this earth. St Patrick's 'Breastplate' (translated and versified by Mrs Alexander, wife of a nineteenth-century Archbishop of Armagh) has a verse about seeking spiritual protection in the things of nature:

> I bind unto myself today
>   The virtues of the starlit heaven,
> The glorious sun's life-giving ray,
>   The whiteness of the moon at even,
> The flashing of the lightning free,
>   The whirling winds' tempestuous shocks,
> The stable earth, the deep salt sea,
>   Around the old eternal rocks;

but it is all seen within the context of the protection afforded by God the Holy Trinity. Celtic lore is beloved of New Agers, but they tend to be very selective in their use of it. St Patrick (and the whole Celtic tradition) had a powerful sense of the closeness of God to the created order, but we must never forget 'the equally powerful sense of the reality – and deceptiveness – of sin and evil which provides its guts and cutting-edge; into which, secondly, is plaited the lovely, essential, redemptive braid of Trinitarian spirituality'.[25]

That shows us that a contemplation of nature should never lead us to cosmic euphoria. There is a dark side, over which we should not allow ourselves to gloss. 'Red in tooth and claw' expresses a truth about the natural order which some advocates of New Age ecology seem to have forgotten. As St Paul well knew, 'the whole created universe in all its parts groans as if in the pains of childbirth' (Rom. 8.22), awaiting its eventual redemption.

Whether this is to be explained in Augustinian terms as a result of the pre-human fall of nature or of part of the angelic creation which thenceforth has acted in Satanic opposition to the loving will of a good God, or whether it is to be explained in Irenaean terms as the inevitable consequence of living in a world which is still early on in the process of creation, is a question for theological disputation. It is a legitimate question, but whatever answer is given, it does not affect the general Christian overview. We cannot blithely sing: 'God's in his heaven: All's right with the world'. We believe that God needed to come out of his heaven and be incarnate because there was so much that was wrong with the world. We cannot therefore read divinity straight from nature, or see nature as divine. It is flawed, as we are. It reflects its Creator, but the waters in which it does so have been stirred, so that what we can see is no more than an imperfect reflection.

Christians therefore cannot wholly go along with New Age insights about the natural world. Nonetheless, the New Age attitude to the earth is calling Christians to a rediscovery of aspects of their faith which they have been in danger of forgetting. If we can reassert them, here at any rate is an area in which the concerns of New Agers and of Christians can be seen as very similar. Those who have been attracted to the New Age because of its environmental stance need not have abandoned Christianity. Perhaps we may be able to win them back!

8
Near Death

New Agers often appeal to the 'near-death experience', or NDE, when they are arguing the case for religion without dogma or spirituality without religion. We need, therefore, to know what the NDE is, why it so often receives a New Age interpretation, and whether that interpretation is the only possible one to put on the experience.

For all its popularity with New Agers, there is nothing particularly new about accounts of the NDE. Written evidence for the phenomenon goes back at least to the days of Plato (427–347 BC). At the close of his book *The Republic*, he told the story of a soldier named Er who was thought to have died on the field of battle, but afterwards revived and told his tale to the amazed bystanders. The Venerable Bede (673–735), in his *History of the English Church and People*,[1] gives an account of what happened to a man called Drycthelm, who was taken through the realms of the next world when he had almost died of a severe illness. Dr Carol Zaleski has worked with a wide range of such accounts, both modern and medieval, and in her book *Otherworld Journeys*, attempts to find out what aspects of them are universal and which are culture-specific.

Few people knew of such stories until the NDE came out of the closet in the mid-1970s, with the publication of Dr Raymond Moody's runaway best-seller *Life after Life*. Since then, a fair-sized library of books has been published on the subject, and an International Association for Near-Death Studies has been formed,[2] with newsletters appearing on both sides of the Atlantic. The Human Sciences Press of New York has, for some years now, issued a quarterly professional *Journal of Near-Death Studies*.

The reason for this explosion of interest in the near-death experience is that advances in medical techniques are making it increasingly possible to revive patients after such traumas as cardiac arrest. At first, people were afraid to report an NDE, and medical and nursing personnel were loath to allow them to talk about it, thinking that it was associated with a psychological abnormality or that it was due to nothing more significant than a florid imagination. There is still much of this attitude around, both in medical and lay circles, but certainly less than there used to be. It is becoming more and more well known that a significant percentage of patients report experiences whilst they are close to death, and that there is a high degree of similarity between different peoples' accounts.

If an NDE is reported, it will usually contain some of the following elements:

The patient feels no pain, but rather a sensation of peace and well-being. He appears to have left his physical body and to be observing it from outside, usually from above, as if he were stuck on the roof of the intensive therapy unit. He does not identify his 'self' with the physical body. That is simply an inert mass of flesh and blood, on and around which the medical team is hard at work, but for which he can not summon up very much interest.

Then he seems to enter a dark tunnel through which he spirals at great speed, often to the accompaniment of loud noises. At the end of the tunnel there is a bright light, into which he emerges. Once he is in the light, he finds himself in surroundings of intense (and almost indescribable) peace. The light is very bright, but it does not hurt his eyes. There may be fields and meadows of a more than earthly greenness, and beautiful streams and waters. All is full of joy and a feeling of love. Out of the light (or sometimes simply *as* the light), a figure appears, which – according to the patient's beliefs – may, perhaps, be identified as God, or Jesus, or the Blessed Virgin Mary, or a patron saint, or Krishna. There may also be family members or departed friends, ready to welcome a new arrival.

The subject reviews his past life, as a 'flashback' or series of flashbacks, and judges himself (or is judged) on the basis of what he has done with his earthly life. There is, however, no feeling of condemnation, only of understanding love. Eventually he moves towards some kind of a barrier; a wall, or a gate, or a door, or a river. He is aware that he cannot cross this, but must go back to earth. So, with reluctance, he turns back and is (usually rapidly and with a sense of shock) back once more in his old, familiar, body, in intense pain, recovering from the accident or cardiac dysfunction which started it all off. But after that, he is usually never again afraid of death or dying.

The picture thus drawn is a composite one from many accounts, and no single story will have all the elements above.

It is notable that nearly all the stories told are of good experiences. Frightening accounts are rare, though they do feature in books on the subject by Dr Maurice Rawlings and Margot Grey. Rawlings believes that they occur as often as good ones, but that they are so unacceptable to the patient that they are almost instantly repressed and never allowed into the conscious mind. Most other researchers in the field disagree, and hold that the bad trip is a genuinely minority experience.

The after-effects include loss of fear of death, an increased feeling of inner spirituality (but a marked reluctance to identify with any kind of institutionalized religious faith), and the desire to spend the rest of one's allotted time doing good to humanity.[3] Often there is a degree of depersonalization, so that it may become difficult to relate to the other members of the family, who can feel that the recovered patient has withdrawn into a private world.

These data are consistent with results obtained in a series of studies by Karlis Osis and Erlendur Haraldsson. They asked questions, not of people who had come close to death and recovered, but of the doctors, nurses, family members, and others who were present at death-beds. In these cases – obviously – the patients themselves could not corroborate the accounts. The most that Osis and Haraldsson were able to do was to interpret the bystanders' accounts of what the patient said and how he behaved.

As we might expect, there is almost no agreement as to the interpretation of the NDE. We shall see in detail before we come to the end of this chapter that New Agers find it easy to interpret it along lines congenial to their beliefs. For that very reason, it is highly suspect to the more conservative of Christians. On the other hand, there are many believers who see the whole phenomenon as consistent with Christian orthodoxy and even as an independent corroboration of Christian teaching. But, as we might expect, there are plenty of medical personnel, psychologists, neurologists, and physiologists, who prefer to explain it entirely within the terms of their particular disciplines.

Reductionist explanations are manifold. The whole experience may simply be a survival strategy. If the body is under intense stress, it may help its chance of survival if it is calm and restful rather than panicky and thrashing about. The NDE lulls the body into relaxation and enables it to conserve its energies for where they are really needed.

There are several possible explanations as to how this may come about. Some people believe that it is simply culturally-determined, so that we remember what we have been told in childhood about heaven, about angels, and about our departed loved ones, and we spin a likely tale out of all this in order to keep us from panicking at the approach of death.

That kind of explanation seems a bit unlikely. It puts too high a value on remembered religious teaching, especially at a time when what is at the top of one's conscious priorities is the immediate emergency rather than remote childhood memories. Dr Melvin Morse, in a study of the NDEs of children, has shown that even small children, too young to have received religious indoctrination, have the same kind of NDE as adults, so that it does not seem likely that our early religious education is responsible for the form of our NDE. There has also been quite a deal of research into the connections between religious and cultural belief–systems and the NDE. This suggests that the experience may be more archetypal than cultural or religious in the narrow sense; but too few cross-cultural studies have so far been done in this area to enable us to do more than guess.

On the other hand, there are psychological factors which seem to predispose certain types of people to the NDE. Kenneth Ring and Christopher Rosing report a preliminary study on this. Many of the NDEers they contacted, had a history of child-abuse or similar trauma in their backgrounds. It may have been that during their childhood, they were motivated to 'tune out' their unpleasant experiences by developing a dissociative trait. In turn, that enabled them to 'tune in' to other non-sensory realities of a psychic type, in the presence of which they felt safer. Accordingly, 'When, in later life such persons undergo the trauma of a near-death incident, they are thus more likely than others, because of their prior familiarity with nonordinary realities, to be able to "flip" into that state of consciousness, which, like a special lens, affords a direct glimpse of the NDE.'[4] Hence, child abuse, psychological dissociation, and psychic sensitivity may be linked with each other and with the NDE. Ring and Rosing stress that this is not a reductionistic view but simply an explanation of the psychological factors behind near-death experiencing.

Some writers have put forward the idea that the NDE is a re-run of the birth experience. As it is being born, the baby travels down a constricting tunnel to the noise of its mother's heart-beat, until it comes out into a place of bright light where it is met by a majestic figure in a white coat. The NDE has the same characteristics. That explanation is not much favoured by those who have studied the NDE. It posits a much more sophisticated perception of birth than would be expected of a neonate. In any case, the birth experience and the death experience are not parallel. The 'figure of light' in an NDE does not pick the newly-dead person up by his heel and smack his bottom until he howls. And, in any case, it has been discovered that people who have been born by Caesarean section are as likely to have NDEs as those who have travelled down a birth canal.

Dr Susan Blackmore, of the Brain and Perception Laboratory at Bristol University, explains the out-of-body experience in psychological terms. We build our 'model of reality', she points out, from the stimuli which bombard us every moment of our lives. The newborn baby is quite incapable of doing this, and it is a long and confusing business for it, gradually, to build up its 'model' of the relation between itself and the outside world. Eventually, most of us, most of the time, accept a 'model of reality' in which our perceiving 'self' sits somewhere in our head, behind our eyes.

But, secondly, consider what happens when we dream. Things that do not surprise us when we are dreaming would terrify us if they happened in waking life. In other words, when we are deprived of sensory input, our 'normal' model of what we imagine the relation between our self and the physical world to be, breaks down and another model takes over. It satisfies us whilst we are in that particular state of consciousness, which is why our dreams seem so real, however bizarre they may be.

Finally, suppose we are in a situation of trauma (as happens when there is cardiac arrest or a severe accident). We are overwhelmed by stimuli which come so fast and so strong that we are not able to process them in the normal way. They may be so overpowering that they contradict our normal model of reality, and we have to revise our ideas of the geographical relation between our 'self' and our body.

We can only work with one model of reality at a time. When we move from waking to dreaming, we change models. The same may happen when the body is under conditions of intolerable stress. The normal model breaks down because the sensory input is too distressing, and the cognitive system has to build the best model it can of the surroundings it thinks it should be seeing. The characteristics of the out-of-body experience are those of a cognitive map of reality based on insufficient sensory data. It is a construct of memory and imagination, and it satisfies us whilst we are in the stressed condition in which it is the only available map. But as soon as the stress is relieved sufficiently for the 'normal' map to take over again, it does so – usually in a fraction of a second, so that we seem to 'flip' from the NDE straight back to a 'normal' perceptive state.

Dr Blackmore's explanation of the out-of-body aspect of the NDE is based on psychological theory. A different account of how the whole NDE may be built up has been provided by two Chilean neurobiologists, Drs Juan Saavedra-Aguilar and Juan Gómez-Jeria.

They believe that a traumatic event such as a serious accident or a cardiac arrest sets up brain stress which results in a release of certain kinds of chemicals and a decrease in the oxygen supply to the brain. This causes discharges in the brain's temporal lobe somewhat similar to those which occur during an epileptic fit. In a detailed review of what all this means in terms of specific neurochemicals and experienced sensation, they show how the de-oxygenation causes loud and unpleasant noises, but the neuropeptides which are then released are responsible for feelings of euphoria and detachment. The epileptiform disturbances bring complex visual hallucinations and the release of memories from earlier life (the 'life review'), whilst the after-discharges cause sensations of brilliant light.

Other neurobiologists, commenting on this scenario,[5] point out that our present knowledge of brain processes is more tentative than the two Chileans seem to allow for. They may be generalizing from insufficient basic data. All the same, their hypothesis is still an 'outstanding workable model', which advancing neurobiological knowledge may well be able either to confirm, to modify, or to disprove.

These explanations do not have to be reductionistic (and the Chileans do not claim that for them). If we explain the chemical and electrical changes in the brain which accompany the NDE, so what? There are chemical and electrical changes accompanying *every* human experience, and we are discovering more about them every year, as the neurobiological understanding of the human brain becomes more extended and accurate.

The Christian believes that God made the world, and that we are part of this world he has made. He also believes that God has made it in one particular way and not in any other. The scientist – yes, even the neurobiologist – is discovering the way in which God has made the world, and he may well wonder at the logic and elegance he discovers within the creation. It would be sheer unintelligent reductionism to say that human beings were 'nothing but' complex neurobiological mechanisms; and sheer unintelligent reductionism to say, when we have discovered the neurobiological concomitants of the NDE (or of any other human experience, from falling in love to listening to a Beethoven quartet) that we have explained that experience without residue. It is still open to us to believe that what Saavedra-Aguilar and Gómez-Jeria are describing is what happens in neuro-biological terms when the immortal soul leaves its physical body behind at the time of death. Christians should welcome neurobiology, as they should welcome all scientific understanding, as telling us more about God's all-but-incredible creation.

So what should we think of the NDE? Some conservative Christians are unhappy about it. It gives people the impression that death is not very serious, and that everything, for everybody, will be all right – whatever their beliefs or previous life-style. The 'figure of light' is not often explicitly connected with Jesus, and it is cosily accepting rather than terrible in aspect and judgemental. For reasons like this, John Weldon and Zola Levitt believe the whole scenario is Satanically-inspired. Testimonies from scientifically-reported death cases and from psychics

> are so identical that there might be some confusion as to the sources, and that, of course, is our point. We think the ultimate source – demon activity – is indeed the same ... We are not totally convinced that the being of light is all he appears to be. Even though he is often interpreted as Jesus himself, or some good angel, we believe he is a sort of demon in disguise ... The devil's chief ploy is just that – to appear as a 'good guy' ... Deception has always been the devil's right hand ... Jesus and the unfallen angels, the scriptures tell us plainly, are concerned about sin and warn unbelievers about the coming judgement. They teach the gospel which sees death as the wages of sin, not a step upwards.[6]

New Age thinkers, on the other hand, have no difficulty in reconciling their beliefs with the data from NDEs.

The out-of-body experience is akin to what seems to be happening to channellers (see Chapter 10 below). It shows the separability of the physical body from the real self, and emphasizes the doctrine that it is the astral or spiritual body which is the more significant.

The new surroundings within which the NDE traveller finds himself are full of light and acceptance. Dr Kenneth Ring points out that in many esoteric traditions, the concept of 'light' is used to describe the 'astral' world or plane, and that in his opinion, 'the idea of an astral reality – or call it whatever else you will – to which we may become sensitive at the point of death is not an outlandish notion, even if it can never be established scientifically.'[7]

The basic optimism of the NDE accords well with New Age teachings about the inherent natural goodness of mankind and the inherent favour which the universe shows towards us.

Some NDEs, however, instead of the flashbacks to scenes of the experient's former life, show what Dr Ring has called 'flash-forwards'.[8] In these, there is a feeling that one is looking at the world's future, and the general tone is one of apocalyptic doom: 'earthquakes, volcanic eruptions, geographical and land-mass upheavals, meteorological disruption, food shortages as a result of droughts, economic breakdown, social unrest, the prevalence of new incurable diseases, possible nuclear war and overall natural holocaust'.[9] This may, of course, signify no more than a collective, almost archetypal, paranoia of a Western world which believes we are on the way to planetary disaster. It could, nonetheless, be harnessed to a belief that the turn of the ages from Pisces to Aquarius will not be achieved without distress.

In the world of the near-death experiencer, there is a feeling of cosmic togetherness. David Lorimer explains the significance of this in his book *Whole in One*, which is subtitled 'The NDE and the ethic of interconnectedness'. His exposition resonates with a great deal of New Age teaching. We might believe that our individual self-consciousness is original and primary, but when 'unitive consciousness is experienced, the boundaries dissolve and there dawns the realization that one's ground is the unitive consciousness field out of which other individual self-consciousnesses also arise: the many arise out of the One and are linked to each other through participation in that One.'[10]

This was the teaching of Plotinus (the third-century philosopher-mystic). It has been taken up in the present century by Paul Brunton, who defined the 'Overself' as the meeting-point between the World-Mind and each conscious being, and held that the Overself is of the same nature as the World-Mind. 'All Overselves exist in the World-Mind just as our thoughts exist in our mind.'[11]

This accords with the New Age idea of the godhead in each one of us. Indeed, Kenneth Ring has suggested that the Being of Light encountered in the NDE is none other than our own higher self:

> In this view, the individual personality is but a split-off fragment of the total self with which it is reunited at the point of death ... This higher self is so awesome, so overwhelming, so loving, and unconditionally accepting (like an all-forgiving mother) and so *foreign* to one's individualized consciousness that one perceives it as *separate* from oneself ... The golden light is actually a reflection of one's own inherent divine nature and symbolizes the higher self. The light one sees, then, is one's own.[12]

The sense which one has in an NDE that one is being sent back to earth for a further stint is of a piece with the belief that this may also happen after a real death. As we shall see in the next chapter, the doctrine of reincarnation is as near as one can get to a belief universal to all New Agers.

And, finally, the way in which NDEers, on their return, frequently espouse a non-sectarian, non-dogmatic, non-institutionalized religion, in which the religious feeling is not tied to any one particular religion but is diffused in a syncretistic way, is characteristic of New Age teachings.

So there is plenty in the NDE which endears it to New Age thinkers. What stance should Christians take to these NDE reports?

The first thing to say is that the NDE happens, and therefore it must be taken seriously. Christians will want to assess it without 'sentimentalism, sensationalism, and spiritualism',[13] but they cannot ignore it, because their faith is a faith based upon the world as it is experienced, not about the world as they might fantasize and wish it to be. We have already seen the three options before us. We can explain it away as a trick of human psychology or as the last wild paroxysms of a brain starved of oxygen and trying to cope with the intolerable. Or we can treat it as a demonic delusion. Or we can take it as a genuine glimpse of the first steps we have to take into a world we shall not fully see until the time for our own death has arrived.

If we are minded to take the third of those options, we do not need to abandon our Christian faith. The NDE is a *near*-death experience. None of the people who have reported it have actually died. For all we know, what they experience may be the delusion which every newly-dead person encounters before the real truth dawns upon them. It could indicate to us that we fool ourselves too readily into believing that our reception into the next phase of our existence is going to be smooth and unthreatening. In any case, at the most, it tells us only about the first few faltering steps into a new dimension. We may extrapolate from this initial glimpse, but if we do so, we must realize that it is easy to make more assumptions than prudence dictates.

Even so tantalizingly brief a glimpse as this, however, has information to give us. What the NDE tells us – if we interpret it positively – is that there can be experiences after death. That in itself is corroboration of a religious standpoint and as such ought not to be sneezed at. It may not specifically confirm particular doctrines which are peculiar to Christianity. For that, we would need a longer look around the territory, and would need to go beyond the frontier post.

The NDE is consistent with the Christian doctrine of the love of God, and of the value to him of the human soul. That in itself is something which needs to be said to the New Ager, who believes that Christianity devalues humanity and that the Christian God is a being full of wrath who enjoys condemning sinners to hell much more than he enjoys welcoming them into heaven. As two recent evangelical writers on the NDE have said, there is in the experience 'an awareness that God, the Supreme Being, is by nature one of love and forgiveness. This is Good News for the fallen, and those who do recover have gone on with a greater openness to God in their lives.'[14]

The fact that the figure of light who is seen in the NDE is not universally interpreted in Christian terms does not mean much. The experience itself is non-verbal, and after it is over, the experiencer has to make verbal sense of it. He will of necessity use terms which are culturally appropriate to his own beliefs. To suppose that this indicates that the whole experience is nothing more than a culturally-determined figment of the imagination is, in the words of Dr Oliver Nichelson,[15] 'much like saying that the red fruit growing on trees is a function of the imagination because it is called "apple" by Americans and "pomme" by the French'.

As for the fact that in the typical NDE, the terrors of judgement are less obvious than the consolations of acceptance, we have already said that this can indicate that God is more favourably-disposed to us than we think we deserve. We might have expected as much from the sayings of Jesus. In the parable of the Labourers in the Vineyard, for example, those who had worked a single hour had as good a reward as those who had sweated all day (Matt. 20.1–16). The thief on the cross was promised a place that day in Paradise (Luke 23.43).

We are so often like the elder brother of the Prodigal Son (Luke 15.11–32). The younger brother returned home after a life of profligacy; his father was overjoyed to see him, but the other brother simply sulked away because he thought the prodigal ought not to have been received so ecstatically. Perhaps God *does* accept sinners. Indeed, if he does not, we are all done for. And if he does, it does not mean that we can all 'sin the more, so that God's grace can the more abound' (Rom. 6.1). It means we can respond to the undeserved love of God by loving him all the more in return. The Christian faith is not about people getting what they deserve. It is about God giving us what we can never deserve. Sin pays a wage, but God gives freely (Rom. 6.23).

So God will never force us into loving him. All he will do is to love and love and keep on loving. If we still reject him, that is our loss. And, if NDEers hold off from keeping company with the rest of Christian believers, and prefer a non-dogmatic and non-organized and non-demanding religion, that is their loss. That is a contingent error of the experiencer, not a necessary corollary of the experience.

In other words, the NDE is patient of a Christian interpretation, and it is not only the New Agers who need to take it seriously.

9
Many Happy Returns

'Is there anybody here who does *not* believe in reincarnation?' The speaker at the College of Psychic Studies had finished his formal lecture, and it was question time. He challenged anybody in the audience of a couple of hundred or so to put their hands up if they didn't hold that particular opinion. One man in the audience mumbled that he wasn't all that sure. Like the coward I am, I kept doggo, telling myself that I was an observer who did not want to influence the event I was watching. Two friends of mine who were present told me afterwards that they were in the same category as I was. But not a hand was raised.

According to opinion polls, a significant minority of the population believes that it has been on earth before. In the UK, it rose from an average of 18% in 1968 to 28% in 1979,[1] and is now, presumably, even higher. The figure in the US is close to a third.[2] At New Age events, my perception is that the percentage rises to within a whisker of 100.

When I wrote a book in the mid-1970s on Christian teaching about life after death, entitled *The Resurrection of Man*, I thought that the doctrine of reincarnation could be summarily dismissed in a couple of pages. By 1984, I was sufficiently convinced of my own ignorance to contribute a whole section of my book *Psychic Studies* to the question. I do not intend to repeat that here, only to comment on the relevance of the idea of reincarnation to a study of the New Age movement. With so substantial a proportion of people holding the doctrine, it is clear that no responsible Christian should fail to think about it. Certainly the amount of recent writing on the subject is daunting. David Lorimer, that incredible polymath, reckoned to have had to consult 75 volumes in order to tackle the chapter on reincarnation in his recent book *Whole in One*. Let any potential writer on the subject beware!

Many people who believe in reincarnation think they are following Hindu or Buddhist thought on the subject. They are probably mistaken. For one thing, the Hindu and Buddhist doctrines of reincarnation are not the same; and for another, the belief in reincarnation which most New Agers hold is neither Hindu nor Buddhist, but a Westernized simplification which is, in one significant respect at least, at variance with both.

The Hindu Upanishads teach that the individual soul or *atman* is an emanation from the supreme and ultimate reality, the transcendent Absolute, *Brahman*. Both *Brahman* and *atman* are indestructible. *Atman* is tied to the wheel of rebirth in a weary cycle of incarnations. 'As a man leaves an old garment and puts on one that is new, the Spirit leaves his mortal body and then puts on one that is new.'[3] He can only achieve release by being identified with *Brahman*. Liberation from the dreaded wheel comes when we can free ourself from the desire of earthly things. We should not be attached either to good works or to their fruits; release will only come by a spirit of entirely selfless love. Meanwhile, there is the law of karma, whereby suffering or enjoyment are the fruit or harvest of one's actions in previous incarnations. What we sow, we reap; what we reap, we must have sowed either in this lifetime or a former one.

The teaching of the Buddha is not the same. His doctrine is a doctrine of impermanence – impermanence not only of the phenomenal world, but even of the individual self. What we take to be the 'self' is simply a temporary aggregate. Rebirth is like carrying a flame from one lamp to another. The flame is the flame of wrong attitudes and desires. What transmigrates is not the self, but karma. 'The karmas of a temporary aggregation, called a particular individual, pass on to another temporary aggregation, which is a different individual.'[4] Thus our action in one lifetime lays down the foundation of the happiness or misery of another individual in another lifetime. Although the Buddha claimed to remember some of his own former incarnations, his teaching was basically of the impermanence of the temporary vessel which carries what it is that incarnates. The goal of life is to extinguish the flame of desires and reach *nirvana*.

Both these bodies of Eastern teaching differ from the typically New Age attitude to reincarnation. It is more common for a New Ager to hold that reincarnation is something to look forward to; it is a case of anticipating 'many happy returns'. Life on this earth is so basically desirable that we want to have other chances of enjoying it. We certainly do not want to escape from the wheel of rebirth. As long as we are on that wheel, things are either good, or they have the potential of being better next time round.

Concepts of reincarnation differ from one New Age teacher to the next, but the commonest Western view is closer to the Hindu than to the Buddhist doctrine. According to it, each of us should expect to return to this earth as a new and total personality; but it will be one which will have some relation to what we are at present. Similarly, our present character and dispositions have been greatly influenced by our past lives. In suitable conditions, we can have access to memories of these former incarnations. If we know what we were in former lifetimes, we can the better understand our present character and behaviour. A belief in reincarnation may also help us live the kind of life which will ensure that, next time, we get a better deal than we are undergoing here and now.

But the idea of reincarnation is not a simple or a monolithic one. Not all believers in it hold that there is an entity called the 'soul' which is immortal and indestructible, and which can be dropped into a series of human bodies one after the other so that it can mature over a series of life-experiences. We have to ask such questions as: 'What is it that reincarnates?' 'What is the meaning of "soul" if it is something which remains continuous throughout a series of incarnations yet cannot normally remember what happened to it in earlier cycles of experience?' 'In what, then, does its continuity between incarnations lie?'

Some people believe that what reincarnates is but a segment of our total self.[5] It is as if we held a peeled orange in our hand, detached a segment from it, and put it onto the table. After a while we returned the first segment and put a different segment of the same orange on the table. Our total self may be a much more complex being than that part of it which is incarnate at this moment. Different segments of it may come to earth at different times, so that when the process is complete, the total self will have been incarnated over a period of many lifetimes, but a particular segment of it may only have enjoyed one earthly life.

Or we may be linked in with a group of souls all of which reincarnate together. Dr Guirdham was a psychiatrist who believed that he and some of his patients had lived as a group of Cathar heretics in southern France in the eleventh century, and were bound to each other by ties which would hold the group together through a series of incarnations.

All this should warn us against oversimplifying our thinking when we are dealing with concepts of reincarnation. Many of the possibilities are described and evaluated in a valuable section of over a hundred pages in John Hick's book *Death and Eternal Life*.

Reincarnation may be argued on empirical grounds as well as by the use of moral arguments. Empirically, it claims support from the existence of 'old souls' in young bodies and of infant geniuses, from the experience of *déjà vu*, from childhood memories of former lives, and from the phenomenon of hypnotic regression. Let us look at these lines of possible evidence one by one.

'Old souls' are people who have learned much from their former lives and, even as children, seem to draw on a greater store of wisdom than that possessed by their parents or teachers. Look at Jesus of Nazareth, a boy of twelve, astounding the doctors of the Law in the Jerusalem Temple and rebuking his parents for their lack of comprehension (Luke 2.41–50). In this view, the same is true of musical geniuses like Mozart – what was a lad of sixteen doing, writing stuff like the *Exsultate jubilate*? And what about those mathematical prodigies who are able to juggle with figures and comprehend the relationships between abstract concepts at an age when they 'ought' not to be able to do so on any 'normal' expectation?

Déjà vu is the (fairly common) experience of feeling, when in a strange place for the first time, that 'I have been here before', and I know what I am going to see when I turn the corner or open the door into the next room. Perhaps I *have* been here before; but not in this present incarnation.

Similar strange memories have been extensively researched by Dr Ian Stevenson. In a typical case, there will be a young child, generally below school age, who claims to remember details of a past life and whose statements can be cross-checked by reference to the families concerned and the locale to which they refer. Over a quarter of a century's painstaking research has led Dr Stevenson to write a series of volumes of 'cases suggestive of reincarnation' – a typically scholarly understatement which claims no more than would be conceded by those who disagree with his interpretation of the data.

As an example, let us take the case of the Pollock twins of Hexham in Northumberland. Joanna and Jaqueline Pollock, aged eleven and six, were killed in a road accident at Hexham in 1957. Seventeen months later, their mother gave birth to a pair of identical twins, Jennifer and Gillian. Jennifer had two birth-marks corresponding to marks on the body of her dead sister Jaqueline. There was a thin white line on her forehead, similar to one which Jaqueline received when she fell off her tricycle at the age of two, and a brown pigmented birthmark on her left hip, identical in shape and position to one which her dead sister had had. There was no similar birthmark on her twin sister. When the twins were four months old, the family moved thirty miles away, to Whitley Bay on the Northumbrian coast. They did not return to Hexham until the twins were three years old. To their parents' amazement, they immediately knew where the school, the playground, and the swings and slides, were, and insisted that they knew the house where they used to live.[6]

Over two thousand similar cases have been documented, of which Dr Stevenson has himself extensively examined 250 and, less extensively, another thousand. The majority are from countries where a belief in reincarnation is an accepted cultural norm, though several are from America and England. Although Dr Stevenson does not think that any single one of the cases he has examined proves reincarnation conclusively, that hypothesis does, in his opinion, offer the best explanation for all the data, collectively viewed.[7]

Many of these cases involve young children whose memories fade during their days at primary school, but there are also cases of 'far memory' involving adults. The majority of adult cases, however, come via the practice of hypnotic regression. People who are sufficiently suggestible can retrieve such ostensible memories almost at will: 'The personalities which emerge during regression are amazingly full-blooded, fluent, and realistic – a Roman matron from third-century Britain, a Jewess in a mediaeval *pogrom*, a Jesuit priest, gutter-urchins and serving-girls. "All human life is there", with a wealth of circumstantial detail.'[8]

In one case of this type, researched by Linda Tarazi and reported in the *Journal* of the American Society for Psychical Research, the subject, a middle-aged American woman, regressed to the character of Antonia. Antonia had lived in Hispaniola, as well as in Spain and elsewhere in Europe, during the sixteenth century. She told a fascinating story of her scrapes with the Inquisition, her hopeless love affair, and her death by drowning off a Caribbean island at the age of thirty-two. 'Hundreds of hours of research over three years in two dozen libraries and universities, travel to Spain, North Africa, and the Caribbean, and correspondence with historians and archivists verified over 100 facts, but uncovered no errors',[9] although, regrettably, Ms Tarazi was never able to discover any independent evidence for the existence of Antonia herself in any of the archives she consulted. Some of the facts could only be checked in sixteenth-century diocesan records in a remote provincial Spanish city, whilst one item was eventually tracked down in the library of the University where the hypnotic subject had attended – but it was in a book in Spanish, over a hundred years old, whose pages had never been cut since its acquisition by the library. In any case, neither normally nor during her regression could the subject either speak, read, or understand Spanish.

What are we to make of all these pieces of data? They are consistent with theories of reincarnation, but they do not demand them. Let us look at the categories again:

We know so little about the normal capacities of the human brain that we do not need to posit any extraordinary cause for the personal or mathematical or musical maturity of those few souls who astonish us with their abilities for wisdom, calculation, or composition.

Déjà vu is a psychological trick which our mind sometimes plays upon us. Various explanations of it have been canvassed.[10]

There are other explanations for claimed past memories, even though some of them may be parapsychological rather than merely psychological. Children may be hoaxing their interlocutors – many of the Indian cases involve children who are trying to claim a higher caste or social class than the one in which they find themselves. Or the people who are regressed may in some strange way be gaining telepathic access to the memories of a departed person whom they then claim is their personal previous incarnation. Or there is the hypothesis of unconscious cryptomnesia. On this supposition, the subject long ago read a book or saw a TV programme or heard someone speaking about a past historic period or a character, and stored the relevant data in their subconscious mind. Under hypnosis, they retrieve those long-lost memories and dress them up into the form of a secondary personality. Dr Reima Kampmann of Finland has investigated a number of such cases,[11] and shown that hypnotic subjects can do this, but that, unfortunately for their reincarnationist beliefs, they provide no correct data beyond those culled from the original distant source, and – more damningly – they faithfully reproduce the errors in the source, thus identifying it beyond cavil.

Then there is the person who creates fantasy 'past lives' as easily as Catherine Cookson produces fictional characters. That may have been what was happening at a day event I attended on 'Past Life Therapy'. It was organized by the Wrekin Trust, the major New Age body in the UK, and led by Dr Roger Woolger. Dr Woolger is a trained psychotherapist and the author of *Other Lives, Other Selves*. For the last fifteen years he has practised Past Life Therapy, which is claimed as 'a highly effective method of focused awareness that enables us to explore and resolve unconscious psychological and emotional patterns which block our full potential'.

Dr Woolger explained that it was not necessary to believe in reincarnation to employ this therapy, but clearly he and the majority of the audience did, and it remains *prima facie* the easiest explanation of what is going on in his sessions.

He works with the 'imagination' – but 'imagination' is not to be understood in its current etiolated meaning of 'the faculty we use when we fantasize something which is not the real case'. Rather, it has to do with the use of images; images which arise from the archetypal depths of the unconscious and have great power in our lives. These images may include apparent memories of events which happened in previous life-times. We *can*, if we wish, think of them as archetypes from the Collective Unconscious of the race which we use in order to diagnose the cause of our present, disabling, emotional dysfunction; but if we treat them as if they were residues of real memories of a real series of past lives, we may get an insight into our present condition which will enable us to remove the block, and have more emotional energy available for living in our present incarnation.

Some people stumble on these apparent memories spontaneously. Some are led to them by realizing that particular places or historical eras are significant for them. Some can gain access to them by flashbacks in dreams, reverie, or trance. Some can be revealed under hypnosis. They can be recognized for what they are because, when we are experiencing them, we do not simply observe the scene as an outsider; we are actually part of it, and emotionally involved as if what is going on is going on to us.

Thus, at Dr Woolger's Study Day, a volunteer from the audience regressed to a former lifetime in which she was a seven-year-old child in a Nazi concentration camp who had become separated from her mother. She found herself in a line of strangers, being led to the gas chamber. In a state of tremendous emotion she cried out piteously for her mother whom she could not find, and, tears streaming down her face, wept her way through the experience of death by poison gas. Then the child who was manifesting in this particular regression was led forward in time to the death of her mother who had survived the war. Apparently, the mother had died in her old age after a long life in which she had had a continuous feeling of guilt at the way in which she had abandoned her child. There was an emotional reunion, and the daughter was able to assure her mother of her forgiveness for the incident which led to the most recent of her deaths.

We were told of other case histories, some of which can be found in detail in Dr Woolger's book. Psychoanalysis sometimes fails to uncover any childhood trauma severe enough to cause a present emotional dysfunction. Complexes *need* not be caused by events happening during childhood. In Dr Woolger's opinion, these cases may be due to the continuing potency of old failures, or humiliations, endured in a previous lifetime. Sometimes quite a mild childhood experience may serve to trigger off an emotional reaction, the real cause of which lies in a former incarnation. The therapy then clears the blocking memories, enables the patient to understand (and therefore to control) his behaviour pattern, and to jettison the disabling material which is preventing him from living life to the full.

Most of Dr Woolger's regressions led to stories of painful or sudden deaths. If we meet our death unprepared, the feelings of fear, or anger, or tension, or humiliation, are locked into the mind and can influence the body in the next lifetime. Thus, a nurse on a children's ward had to have open heart surgery. When regressed, she acted out the story of an Aztec priest (frequently, patients regress to be of the other sex). The work of this Aztec involved sacrificing children. Revolted by what he had to do, he refused to continue, whereat his fellow-priests put him to death by tearing his heart out. By her care for children, the nurse was compensating in this life for her earlier wickednesses, but the surgery she had to undergo brought back memories of the way in which she had previously died.

Phobias may have a past-life origin. People afraid of flying may have been shot down during the war when they were piloting an aircraft. Those who suffered from famine last time round may be over-careful about wasting food now – or they may compensate by compulsive overeating. A Caesarean birth may be a mother punishing her own body for the sin of using a knife to sacrifice children in the past life. Arthritis (frequently psycho-somatic) may be caused by the memory of a life as an ascetic who thought he did not deserve pleasure, so took it out on the body. The office workaholic who feels she will not be respected if she doesn't deliver the goods may be the reincarnation of a warrior who refused to fight, and thereby disgraced both himself and his captain. In this life she has become a person who is trying desperately to live so as not to let either herself or her boss down. And so on, and so on.

But – again – there is more than one explanation of all these data. The *prima facie* reason may not be the real one. Perhaps open-heart surgery led the nurse to a fantasy of having had the heart ripped out. It is surprising how many of Dr Woolger's patients were Aztecs who sacrificed children, or medieval warriors who killed and raped and pillaged. There seems to be something more archetypal than historical at work here.

Maybe the explanation lies in the mechanism of projection. If there is something about ourselves which we cannot consciously acknowledge to be our fault, it is easier to project it onto some other person or entity – as happened on the earliest such occasion, when Adam blamed Eve and Eve blamed the serpent. 'It wasn't me; it was something that got into me.' Someone who is afraid of flying thinks that the phobia shows him to be a wimp. He does not like the self-image that this behaviour brings. The fantasy of having been a fighter pilot over wartime Germany enables him to pass the blame for his phobia from his present self on to someone else (albeit someone who he was at an earlier stage). It is a less self-threatening explanation than the one which sees the present personality as defective in some way. By thus distancing our present selves from blame, we can give ourselves permission to do something about the behaviour that is crippling us.

Whatever the explanation, the healing is *real* – Dr Woolger is a successful psychotherapist, and his patients are rightly grateful to him for the help he has given in rescuing them from an intolerable life. But whether healing comes from genuine reconciliation with a past-life personality or whether Dr Woolger is simply colluding with the mistaken beliefs of his patients, is the great unanswered question. Those of us who do not believe that reincarnation is the reason for his successes have no difficulty in looking elsewhere for a satisfactory explanation.

But whatever form of the reincarnation doctrine an individual may embrace, why is it so attractive? For some, it is because it coheres with their experience of nature's cycle of the annual death and rebirth of vegetation, and thereby puts the human soul within a larger and more universal pattern. But this is not its main attraction. Reincarnation appeals, I believe, largely because it gives people a satisfying reason for the inequities and iniquities of the world around them; but partly, also, because, although many people cannot believe that after this present life they will simply cease to be, they are not capable of conceiving any better place to continue their existence than here on this earth.

The concept of karma seems to them to be a morally fair reason for the fact that some people come into the world physically handicapped or within a disadvantaged culture. Such people may have deserved their misfortune because of their past-life wrong-doings (remember the question asked of Jesus in John 9.2, 'Had this man sinned [before his birth], that he was born blind?').

> The universal law of karma ... is that of action and reaction, sowing and reaping. In the course of natural righteousness, man, by his thoughts and actions, becomes the arbiter of his destiny. Whatever energies he himself sets in motion must return to him as their activator. An understanding of karma as the law of justice underlying life's inequalities serves to free the human mind from resentment against God and man.[12]

This concept also provides us with a purely self-regarding reason for present-day ecological and political awareness. If we pollute the earth, or allow tyrants to remain unchallenged, we shall only return to experience in our next lifetime the results of our folly this time around.

It does not matter that we cannot normally remember the former lifetime which has so shaped our position in this. Some of the appropriate memories may be accessible given the right technique for reactivating them, and even if they are not, the existence of a former lifetime provides sufficient reason for our present woes, and is ready to hand.

There is an alternative explanation for present misfortunes, which is that those who suffer them are 'advanced souls' who need to have this testing experience in order the further to purify themselves. (Scientific explanations, in order to be valid, have to be falsifiable, and karma therefore does not qualify as a scientific one, since no possible data could prove it wrong. But in this it is on all fours with most explanations of a religious kind – Christian or others.)

Either way, as David Lorimer points out, the doctrine of karma is no excuse for 'a hard-hearted refusal to help others on the grounds that they deserve their misfortunes'. Such a repulsive attitude 'can only serve to entangle ourselves in the karmic web'.[13] We are on this earth in order to better it as well as ourselves.

The doctrine of karma is one way of trying to 'justify God's ways to man'. The effort has long exercised religious thinkers. Some theologians use the concept of Satan to justify the unfairness of this world.[14] Others emphasize that we are in a world still 'in the making', and we may therefore expect imperfections to be endemic within it. The problem has spawned a whole library of books, and we have not got the space here to go into it. John Hick's *Evil and the God of Love* is an excellent introduction to the complexities of the whole subject. Suffice it to say that a doctrine of reincarnation is not the only way out of this metaphysical maze.

Reincarnation has also been defended on the grounds that it is fairer than the doctrine that we are sent for ever either to heaven or hell for our conduct in one brief human life. It is unethical, say the reincarnationists, to offer so disproportionate a reward or punishment for a life which may have lasted for only a few days, or which may have placed us in circumstances in which it was impossible to believe in God or to live in a morally acceptable way. So it is. But the doctrine of a future life which is a matter of reward or punishment rather than the result of the undeserved grace of a generous God, is not defensibly Christian. Some form of it may have been held in past ages or even (for all I know) may still be held in some circles today. I do not hold it, nor do I see it as part of my brief for Christianity to try to defend the indefensible.

Another argument for reincarnation is the conviction that one lifetime is not long enough to learn all the lessons a soul needs to have mastered if it is to progress, nor one historical era and cultural *milieu* enough to give a soul a wide enough selection of experiences. People who believe in reincarnation are often those who feel they have had a raw deal in life, and would like to have another chance in more propitious circumstances. Joseph Addison's optimistic expectation that

> Through every period of my life
> Thy goodness I'll pursue,
> And after death in distant worlds
> The glorious theme renew

does not satisfy them. They wish for more experience in *this* world, not in a series of distant ones. The Christian doctrine of eternal life does not catch their imagination. They think it either unintelligible or boring; or else unworthy, because they believe they need more moral growth before they are ready for any beatific vision.

For this, perhaps Christians have only themselves to blame. In recent years they have tended to lay more stress on putting this present world to rights than in teaching their members anything about another one. They were right in what they affirmed, but ill-advised in what they left unemphasized. It is time for the pendulum to swing back. Not to the sometimes sickly and immoral sentimentality of an earlier century, but to something which can be understood as intellectually convincing, morally right, and emotionally worth investing in. We have overemphasized the idea of heaven as a place or state of rest and achievement, of contemplative and static perfection, and failed to speak often enough or confidently enough of it as a place of continuing exploration into God and growth in grace.

So we need a better understanding of the Christian doctrines, both of earth and what lies beyond it. We need to affirm that this world is a marvellous world, sadly in need of all the friends it can get, but still potentially a place of glory. But we need also to teach that if our sight is limited to it and our souls inextricably bound to it, we are failing to enthuse our hearers about the possibilities of learning, growing, and experiencing in an even more breathtaking environment. We need to affirm, with the reincarnationists, that there is more to learn than one earthly lifetime can teach us. But this one lifetime may be a launching-pad for others where we shall see and experience things beyond human sight and beyond earthly hearing and beyond our present limited comprehension. It is not simply a treadmill to which we are condemned to return age after age for more of the same thing if we have not qualified for anything better. God has better things in store for us; things that will boggle our imagination!

There is, in New Age circles, a persistent fantasy that reincarnation was standard Christian doctrine until it was condemned by two Councils at Constantinople in the middle of the sixth century. The story goes that those Councils, conducted with all the consummate skulduggery we associate with the ecclesiastico-political manoeuvrings of the Byzantine empire, outlawed a doctrine which up till then was fully permissible and, indeed, orthodox. From then on, reincarnation was out-of-bounds to Christian theologians, which is why we no longer hear it from our pulpits. Only today, in our more relaxed and pluralistic society, may we once more ask questions that lead us back to those lost but primitive Christian doctrines.

We may wonder why reincarnationists should want to legitimate their doctrine in this particular way. In fact it is all part of a larger New Age pattern. As we have already seen in other contexts, the New Agers wish to reverse the evils of this technological age and return to the authority of a deeper wisdom of a simpler past. Some New Agers believe that this deeper wisdom may be found by returning to such civilizations as ancient Egypt, or pre-Columbian America, or lost Atlantis, or mythical Lemuria. Others, however, believe it resided in a lost age of the Christian Church before it became corrupted by the changes which have culminated in our present dire position. They have a kind of love/hate relationship with the Church. They cannot be doing with it as it is, but they do not want to be doing without it, because they believe that if only it would preach their beliefs, it could once more become a powerful tool for the spiritualization of the whole globe.

So all sorts of beliefs are predicated of a supposed early Church which was subsequently corrupted by misguided theologians or power-seeking clerics. According to some hypotheses, this happened when the Councils of Constantinople outlawed reincarnation, or even earlier, when the Roman Empire became Christianized under Constantine in the fourth century. According to others, it happened right at the beginning, when that arch-heretic Paul changed the pure and simple gospel of Jesus into a salvation-mystery like so many other religions of the Roman Empire.

Hence we get New Age reconstructions of the original gospel. Jesus was 'really' a medium, or a vegetarian, or an Egyptian wonderworker, or a guru who escaped death on the cross and went to Kashmir where his tomb may be seen to this day; Jesus was a Gnostic, Jesus was an Essene (never mind that what scholars are rediscovering about the Gnostics or the Essenes is quite unlike what New Agers think – the Gnostics or the Essenes could have been as corrupt as the early Church and subsequently as transmogrified).

So the idea of Jesus as a teacher of reincarnation is all of a piece with these other samples of New Age reinterpretation. Douglas Groothuis has recently catalogued some of them, and provided a useful critique, in his book *Revealing the New Age Jesus*. But it is all fantasy:

> New Age inclinations to the contrary, the Canon of the New Testament is not an ad hoc collection of material created to suppress legitimate documents that present a New Age version of Jesus. No one should reject the biblical presentation of Jesus on

the basis that the books of the New Testament were merely a result of political or theological prejudice. That idea simply does not bear historical scrutiny.[15]

The New Testament as a whole gives us no grounds for believing that Christians of the first generation could conceivably have held reincarnation as a possible option. Their dominant thought (see, for example, Mark 13.30; John 21.22; 1 Thess. 4.15; 2 Peter 3.3–10) was that the world would come to an end in the lifetime of the majority of them. There would simply not be any time left for further incarnations. The idea which runs through the New Testament is not reincarnation but resurrection – Christ's as first-fruits, and the resurrection of believers as a consequence.

As the Christian centuries passed by, the faith had to make its way in the world of Greek and Hellenistic philosophy, and the Christian Fathers needed to define their position in relation to the pervasive ideas of the Mediterranean thinkers of their day. So, naturally, some of them toyed with the idea of reincarnation. But the most that even the boldest of them felt able to affirm was that the soul may not have been created at the moment of conception or birth, but that it might have pre-existed. Not, however, as an earthly incarnation, but in some heavenly, pre-mundane, realm. As Wordsworth was to write many centuries later,

> ... trailing clouds of glory do we come
> From God who is our home.[16]

The most influential such thinker was Origen, in the first half of the third century. He was finally condemned, three hundred years later, at the two Councils held in Constantinople in 543 and 553, but not for teaching reincarnation – a doctrine he had never espoused. The true facts are well stated, and the evidence marshalled, by Professor John Hick in an important extended Note on pages 392–4 of his book *Death and Eternal Life*. 'Reincarnation', he concludes, was taught, not by the early Christians, but

within the gnostic movement from which the church early distinguished itself and then treated as a dangerous foe ... Origen affirms the pre-existence of the soul and regards the fortunate and unfortunate circumstances of birth – for example, as healthy or deformed – as rewards and punishments for virtue and sin in the soul's previous existence ... However, this previous existence was not on earth but in the heavens, and did not constitute one of a series of former lives. Origen does not speak of successive incarnations of the soul in different earthly bodies but only of the soul's pre-existence in some higher realm prior to its descent into this world.

The Constantinople Councils declared belief in 'the fabulous pre-existence of souls' to be worthy of anathema, but made no mention of reincarnation.

So I still hold by what I wrote in 1984:

> Those who would have us believe that reincarnation was an accepted belief in the early Church ... are misreading the evidence. Speculations about reincarnation were attempts to make of Christianity what it did not profess to be, and they were entertained only by an unrepresentative minority of thinkers. They were unceremoniously thrown out, but they were never likely to have converted the Church as a whole. Those who today try to persuade Christians of the truth of reincarnation cannot credibly claim that they are restoring an ancient Christian doctrine to its true place. They are following in the wake of idiosyncratic thinkers who were never able to persuade the bulk of Christianity to their way of looking at things.[17]

10
Open Channels

I first heard Saint Bartholomew talking when I was attending an event in St James's Church, Piccadilly. He spoke through Joy Balles-Beeson, an American minister of what she described as a 'metaphysical Church'. Joy told us that she had been channelling Bartholomew for the last eight years; which she then proceeded to do.

If she was in trance, it was a very light one. She told us that she would have very little recollection afterwards of the precise material she would be channelling. Truth to tell, it was unmemorable also to those who listened to it for about thirty minutes. We are all light-bearers, Bartholomew told us. There is no such thing as real darkness, only the blocking of the light. Within, we all know that we are of the light, and through us the energy of this planet is being raised. We are becoming closer to spirit than we were beforehand. Each of us is part of a soul-group which pre-existed our present incarnation, at a time when we lived before, either on this earth or on another planet. And there was much more, in the same vein.

Was it Bartholomew the Apostle who was speaking to us through Joy? Or was it Joy herself on a public ego-trip? Or was there an amalgam of the two, with the ideas of Bartholomew being refracted and changed by the cultural background and the ideas and assumptions of the person who was acting as his channel? Or was something more sinister going on, and were we listening, not to Bartholomew at all, but some other discarnate spirit? The ideas being put forward were not reminiscent of the kind of teaching that was characteristic of the early Christian Church. So, were the ideas which were being put forward divine truth or demonic error?

I could not help but irreverently recall those wicked verses of Eric Mascall which were going the rounds in the days when I was a young curate. New Testament scholars of an earlier generation had worked out that Nathanael, sitting under a fig tree and mentioned in St John's Gospel as 'an Israelite indeed, in whom there is no guile', was the same person as the disciple Bartholomew who appears in the other three Gospels. But more modern scholarship divides the Gospels into sources to which it gives distinguishing letters, and makes the identification very uncertain. So Dr Mascall wrote that

> Beneath a fig-tree once there sat
> A very guileless Jew.
> He had the firm conviction that
> He was Bartholomew.
>
> But then the Higher Critics came,
> With L and M and Q,
> And if you ask him now his name
> He hasn't got a clue.[1]

I felt that, however firmly Joy Balles-Beeson held the conviction that the entity speaking through her was Bartholomew, the rest of us didn't have much of a clue about who he really was. Certainly, had he been who he claimed to be, I could not imagine his addressing a couple of hundred people gathered in a church building and not once in the course of thirty minutes mentioning either God or Jesus. A retired professional man was once told by a communicating spirit that 'the gatherings we have, produce unclouded thought of an exalted nature'.[2] It didn't seem to be happening that night.

'Channelling' as a phenomenon is highly popular in New Age circles. What is happening when it takes place? And what should Christians think about it? Anyone who is familiar with Spiritualism will see the similarity to (and the differences from) what goes on in that *milieu*. What is the relation between the two?

Spiritualism as a modern religion began about 150 years ago. Rappings were heard in a house in New York state by two young sisters, who interpreted them as the work of communicating spirits. They provided the catalyst for the promulgation of a new religion on which Andrew Jackson Davies and others had been working for some time,[3] and the movement spread like a prairie fire – in the United States and beyond – until it had affected an incredible range of followers from cottagers to courtiers. The story gained credence that even Queen Victoria herself had taken part in sittings in which her faithful retainer John Brown acted as the medium whereby she retained contact with the spirit of her beloved Prince Albert. Unlikely as that was, the claim still reappears every now and again in Spiritualist books and newspapers. On the other side of the Atlantic, Abraham Lincoln was advised from time to time in his conduct of the Civil War by a trance medium named Nettie Colburn, to whom he had been introduced by his wife.[4] The spectacle of an astrologer at the White House is not without precedent.

Relationships between Spiritualism and Christianity have always been uneasy. Some people see Spiritualism as a proof of the immortality of the human soul. For them, this is a scientific matter rather than a religious claim. It has been empirically verified for them in the séance-room and it has no necessary connection with any belief in God. For many years, under its former editor, *Psychic News* used to thrive on snide references to Christianity. Not only, so it said, did Christians espouse a faith which was without proof; they also wilfully rejected such proof of life after death as Spiritualism was able to provide. The Spiritualists' National Union since 1987 has forbidden new Spiritualist churches which become affiliated to it to use 'the trappings of other religions', on the grounds that 'Christian symbols [are] not acceptable to non-Christians and [are] liable to create, through association, a Christian identity in the minds of those who [come] into their churches'.[5] At least we know where we stand.

Other Spiritualists retain the epithet 'Christian', but continue to be held at arm's length by the mainstream churches. The Greater World Christian Spiritualist Association was founded by Winifred Moyes sixty years ago. It has as its objects:

> to spread in all directions the truth of survival after death, of spirit communion, of healing by the power of the Holy Spirit and to disseminate the teachings received from highly evolved spirit messengers.

Its mission is 'to proclaim the indivisibility of Christianity and Spiritualism' and to reinterpret the Bible, and especially the gospel story, in a spiritualistic light. Christian Spiritualism is eclectic and syncretistic. It 'does not invite anyone to turn their back on the religion of their choice, but leaves its doors open to all investigators and seekers of spiritual truths'.

White Eagle Lodge, redolent of the beliefs of a strong-minded upper-middle-class Englishwoman of the between-the-wars vintage, is a hybrid between Spiritualism and Theosophy, with Christian overtones. As with Theosophy, there is a private inner esoteric group within the movement. 'White Eagle', who was said to have lived on a mountain in the East, and to be one of the 'brothers of the Great White Light in the world of spirit', gave messages to the founder of the Lodge, Grace Cooke, between 1929 and 1979. The opening of its 'first temple of the New Age' in 1974 was accompanied by Bach chorales, excerpts from Brahms' *German Requiem*, Parry's setting of Blake's *Jerusalem*, and a rendering of 'All people that on earth do dwell'.[6] White Eagle Lodge teaches reincarnation, speaks of the coming of the Christ Light into man's heart, and avers that Jesus 'danced the joyful dance of spiritual freedom'. But there is little in its teachings which seems distinctive of Christianity. God is the Great White Spirit, and the messages of White Eagle are fuller of moral uplift and comfortable teachings about the after-life than of what Christians would recognize as theology.

To come closer to orthodox Christianity, Spiritual Frontiers Fellowship International was founded by a group of Christian ministers and lay-people from the major American denominations in 1956 as a means of working towards some kind of reconciliation between the churches and psychics. It also sponsors an 'academic affiliate' known as the Academy of Religion and Psychical Research, which publishes a quarterly learned journal, the *Journal of Religion and Psychical Research*.[7]

The heyday of Spiritual Frontiers Fellowship was in the 1960s when its protégé, the medium Arthur Ford, appeared on Canadian television with the Anglican bishop James Pike.[8] According to its constitution, the Fellowship was established 'to sponsor, explore and interpret the growing interest in psychic phenomena and mystical experience within the church', with, as its goal, 'the development of spiritual growth in the individual and the encouragement of new dimensions of spiritual experience within the church'. As founded, it was 'Christian in origin and emphasis, interdenominational in scope, and inter-faith in pursuit of its ultimate goal'. I was present at its 1991 Annual Conference in North Carolina and privileged on that occasion to attend its Council meeting, which went on for two-and-a-half days.

There are no doctrinal conditions for membership either of the Fellowship or its Council, and it is at present engaged on a very active drive to increase its membership. There is therefore nothing to guarantee its continued orthodoxy within Christianity. It could become as marginally Christian as some of the groups we have already discussed, and its influence on the major American Christian denominations could become even less than its present low profile. Certainly nowadays it plays its inter-faith card more obviously than its Christian ecumenical one, and has a strong New Age flavour.

Thus, the brochure for its 1991 National Conference found great difficulty in mentioning God, preferring such phrases as 'The One behind The Order of the World', who is 'One we now recognize as the Divine and/or Universal Mind, the One, the All of which we are made'. This may, of course, be an attempt to cast its net more widely and to appeal to those who are frightened away by signs of Christian dogmatism. But it does not serve to endear it to those who wish to remain firmly within the Christian Church whilst exploring their psychic potential.

By contrast, the Churches' Fellowship for Psychical and Spiritual Studies[9] seeks to be solidly grounded within orthodox Christianity. Founded in England in 1953 as The Churches' Fellowship for Psychical Study, it changed its name to the present form ten years later. By the mid-1970s, its Patrons included nine Anglican diocesan bishops 'and others prominent in the Church, Science and Public Life'. Associate and non-voting membership requires no doctrinal declaration, but full members have either to be practising members of a Christian Church which belongs or is affiliated to the World Council of Churches, or must acknowledge Jesus Christ as Lord and Saviour of the World. There is a sister body, the CFPSS (Scotland), with a similar constitution.

The Fellowship seeks to nurture Christians who accept their psychic ability as a gift from God. It is a gift which needs to be hallowed and directed aright, as part (but only part, and not the determinative part) of their Christian discipleship. Unsought psychic experiences need to be evaluated in a discerning spirit. They may be benign, malign, or neutral. Even if they are benign or neutral, it is easy to be thrown off balance by them, and balance is an essential part of mature Christian discipleship. Too many people have become monomaniac bores after a psychic experience, and are no advertisement for a sane Christian life.

Whilst the Fellowship does not forbid resort to mediums, it points out that mediumship

can be a dangerous gift and should be consciously used only with great caution and only for a good purpose. Those who are mentally or psychologically unstable should not seek to employ the gift. Everyone should know that deliberately induced psychic awareness is the result of deliberately laying oneself open to psychic influences and that some psychic influences are evil. Deliberately induced psychic awareness should be undertaken only with prayer and with a good intent. Idle curiosity and levity are completely out of place and dangerous. The good intent may be either the serious intent to advance scientific knowledge or the intent to help others.[10]

It is a way by which some people may be assured of the survival of their loved ones, after which they can leave them in God's hands and not hinder them (or be themselves hindered) in their continuing spiritual journey.

A Committee appointed by the then Archbishop of Canterbury reported on Spiritualism in 1939, although the Bishops' Meeting that year (and subsequently) decided not to publish their findings or endorse their recommendations, and they were not fully made public until the forty-year embargo on them had run its course. The CFPSS disavows Spiritualism as a religion, but on mediumistic practices would probably agree with the majority recommendation of the 1939 Committee that 'those who have the assurance that they have been in touch with their departed friends may rightly accept the sense of enlargement and of unbroken fellowship which it brings'.[11]

Many people, however, find that resort to mediums is a spiritual cul-de-sac. The CFPSS would not argue against them. Those who rely on this kind of communication may find that their grieving and the process of their bereavement becomes permanently stalled in what should be an early stage of its natural course. That, at any rate, is the frequent experience of counsellors for Cruse–Bereavement Care. They know that if their clients find a home within Spiritualism, it is often hard to move them on to a position where the process of grieving can continue and a normal emotional life can re-emerge from the shadow of the bereavement trauma.

But Spiritualism is not New Age. New Agers regard the typical Spiritualist demonstration as very old hat indeed. They are not particularly interested in messages from Aunt Matilda telling us that she is alive and well and in the spirit world and that she is keeping a watching eye on all that we are doing here below. They would say that Spiritualists deal primarily with the psychic, and the psychic is not the spiritual. Christians would agree, and would go on to say that the 'psychic' deals with the (not necessarily redeemed) human soul or 'psyche', whereas the 'spiritual' is concerned with humanity as it is transformed by the touch of God's Holy Spirit. Many Spiritualists are materially or psychically oriented, and are remarkably unspiritual. Not all, however. There are communicators and communicators.

The more spiritually-minded Spiritualists allow that what they term the 'lower' communications are necessary to help a certain kind of follower at a certain stage of spiritual growth, but they do not set much store by them. Paul Beard, for example, in his trilogy of books on the nature of man, God, and reality as revealed by spirit communications,[12] builds up a picture which depends on information of a much more metaphysical nature than those messages characteristic of the late Doris Stokes.[13]

Which brings us to 'channelling', the term much more in fashion than 'mediumship', and a phenomenon which the New Age has taken to itself in a big way.[14]

Channellers are similar in many respects to those mediums who purport to work through 'guides' or 'controls' rather than bringing messages direct from the relatives their clients wish to contact. There is thus a chain which runs from the deceased loved one, via the disembodied spirit who acts as the control, and through the medium herself, before the message reaches the client. 'Chan', the guide or control of Mrs Ivy Northage, tells her to inform her sitters that their loved ones 'seldom communicate on their own behalf, they relay what they would have the guide convey through the mind of the medium'.[15]

The significant difference between Spiritualist mediums with their controls and New Age channellers is that the New Age channellers are not interested in relaying mundane messages for private clients. Their controls are exalted spirits (human or other) who offer help, counsel, and guidance to the whole of the human race.

Thus, the Greater World Christian Spiritualist Association relies largely on an entity named Zodiac who claims to have been a teacher in the Temple at Jerusalem in the time of Jesus. Zodiac returned to earth in order to communicate through Winifred Moyes as his channel, and used her in this way for over thirty years. As a celestial messenger entrusted with a special mission, he brought spiritual truths to mankind. They included 'the perfect justice of divine laws', 'the divinity within ourselves', and 'progression through loving service' – a 'faith based on morality'.

Theological sophisticates who hear this will murmur to themselves the word 'Pelagianism'. Pelagius was a British monk of the fourth century who believed that human effort was rewarded with divine grace. Augustine opposed him, and taught that what came first was not our effort, but that we needed God's initiative of grace before we could even have the desire to do good. In terms of formal theology,

Augustine won; but as far as popular thought was concerned (especially in Britain), the Pelagian system has gone unchallenged for centuries. Pelagians urge us to try to raise ourselves to the heavenly realms by tugging at our own bootstraps. That kind of exhortation is a favourite amongst amateur English moralists, but it has nothing at all to do with the Christian doctrine of the justification of sinful humans by the grace of God through faith in Jesus as the incarnate, crucified, and risen Saviour.

It should not surprise us to be told that this kind of teaching has come from a Jewish rabbinic contemporary of Jesus of Nazareth who was not one of his followers. What is saddening is that such a spirit should be regarded as a suitable guide for an organization which claims to be *Christian* as well as Spiritualist.

Each channeller has her or his own tutelary spirit. Sometimes it is an anonymous ancient from some particular historical place and period who, because his real name is either unimportant or unknown, is given an invented name by the channeller. Thus, we can hardly believe that a teacher in the Jerusalem Temple in the first century AD would really have been named Zodiac. He has been given that name simply (so we are told) because 'he was chosen to lift man's thoughts heavenwards'.

Perhaps the three channelled entities most influential in current New Age circles are Seth, Ramtha, and Lazaris.

Seth[16] was channelled – originally by ouija board, then clairaudiently, then in light trance, and finally in full trance – through a thirty-four-year-old aspiring poet and novelist named Jane Roberts from 1963 until her death in 1984. He taught that 'we are individualized portions of energy, materialized within physical existence, to learn to form ideas from energy, and to make them physical'.[17] He described himself as 'an energy personality essence no longer focused in physical reality' and was responsible for at least eight books of channelled material as well as interpretative literature written by Jane Roberts herself in her normal state of consciousness.

Ms J. Z. ('Jayzee') Knight's 'Ramtha', 'The Enlightened One', is supposed to be a 35,000-year-old warrior king from the lost island of Lemuria. He was unkindly described by Marcello Truzzi as acting 'like a third-rate impression of Yul Brynner in a road tour of *The King and I*'.[18] That does not stop Ms Knight discovering that Ramtha is a very lucrative lodger in her skull. Channelling can be very big business, and with Ms Knight, it does not come cheap.

Similarly with Lazaris. The name belongs to an entity channelled by Jach Pursel since 1974, who teaches us '*how* to be powerful . . . *how* to change our lives and then teaches us specific techniques to accomplish the change'.[19] The Lazaris enterprise is a highly profitable corporation in which a 'mailroom, and a row of computer workstations and telephones are manned by staff members each day'.[20]

Other channelled spirits are believed to come from ancient civilizations which were characterized by a deep spirituality which has been lost to the world until now. Favourite candidates are ancient Egypt, American Indian native culture, or the Celtic world of earlier Britain. Sometimes (like the 'devas' of Findhorn) they are nature spirits. Some of them are advanced souls at a higher plane of evolution than we earthlings have yet achieved. One spirit channelled through a Danish sensitive even claimed to be the entity 'historically known as Satan'.[21] (Conservative Evangelicals would presumably regard that as a rare moment of candour.) Jon Klimo tells us[22] that 'space brothers' are highly popular. I once met a woman doctor from Finland who claimed to have been contacted and taught by creatures from an Unidentified Flying Object. One channelling spirit claims to have been the wife of Socrates.[23] In New Zealand in the mid-1970s I met a clergyman who channelled from St Stephen the first Christian martyr.[24]

One of the most influential books of channelled material, certainly for New Agers, is *A Course in Miracles*. Its contents were given over a number of years through Helen Schucman, a psychologist employed at Columbia University College of Physicians and Surgeons in New York. It was published in 1975, ten years after the first message was received, and has since sold in its hundreds of thousands. The main 'course' consists of 365 extracts covering over 1200 pages, arranged as daily inspirational reading for a year. From whom was it channelled? We are assured that: 'The name of Jesus Christ as such is but a symbol. But . . . it is a symbol that is safely used as a replacement for the many names of all the gods to which you pray . . . This course has come from him.'[25]

If that be true, then Jesus has become incredibly verbose in his New Age. And his style has changed. The historical Jesus was full of puzzlingly ambiguous sayings, and equally puzzling but lively and close-to-nature stories and parables. Yes, ambiguous. We still argue over what that term 'Son of Man' means (and whether it is 'Son of Man' with a capital M, or 'Son of man' with a small one), or what the Kingdom of God (or Kingdom of Heaven) really is, or what the precise point of a parable was, or what it was told in order to teach. That is the genius of the Jesus of the Gospels. He has a rare capacity for setting thought in motion – but it is *our* thought, not an interpretation which *he* foists upon us. We have to do our own puzzling out. And, as an educational method, that takes a great deal of beating.

A Course in Miracles is different. We get turgid passages such as

> There is nothing outside you. That is what you must ultimately learn, for it is the realization that the kingdom of Heaven is restored to you. For God created only this, and he did not depart from it nor leave it separate from Himself . . . [Heaven] is merely the awareness of perfect oneness, and the knowledge that there is nothing else; nothing outside this oneness, and nothing else within.[26]

An Evangelical book on Satanism I once came across,[27] bade me to persevere with it, even though 'Satan does not want you to read this material! . . . He will afflict you with overwhelming sleepiness'. Certainly I was overwhelmed with a similar feeling as I tried to plough through the text of the *Course*, which I found almost totally unreadable. It is only fair to say, however, that people who have taken it as their 'inspirational reading' are loud in its praises, and teachers who use it emphasize that students should take the full year over it and not read more than one day's worth of text at a time.

Schucman is not the only person to claim direct inspiration from Jesus. Christians from all the mainstream Churches believe that he speaks to them and gives them guidance for their lives. Usually such guidance comes as an inner conviction after prayerful wrestling with the problems besetting the Christian believer, but occasionally it is given in more dramatic ways. Judith Pinhey, a devout and orthodox Christian who would, I am sure, want to have nothing to do with the New Age, believes that she has heard the voice of Jesus speaking directly and out loud to her, and in her book *The Music of Love*, she offers her readers nearly a hundred short passages which she has received in this manner. They have been selected from a larger number by Robert Llewelyn of the Julian shrine at Norwich. He sees them as similar to what he terms the 'imaginative locutions' received by Julian of Norwich or Teresa of Avila. Before we accept them at face value, we need to ask some searching questions about them. As with the Marian visions of Medjugorje and elsewhere, we need to be very cautious in attributing divine authority to words which have been inwardly heard. (After all, Peter Sutcliffe became the 'Yorkshire Ripper' because of the words he heard inwardly.) The message needs to be legitimated. This is not done by saying that the method by which it has been received puts it beyond criticism. It is done by testing its contents against received Christian teaching.

But the 'locutions' of Judith Pinhey and other Christians are not 'channelled' material. They are akin to meditations on Christian truth by persons who believe that Jesus can still speak to his disciples today. New Age channelled material which claims to come from Jesus is not a bit like Judith Pinhey's messages. For example, Ken Carey recorded the following on one occasion: 'I am Christ. I am coming this day through the atmosphere of your consciousness . . . I came to you first through a man named Jesus . . . Whoever will come after me will have to . . . follow along the lines of my vibrational field'.[28] But then, for New Agers, 'Jesus' and 'Christ' are not necessarily synonyms. As the *Manual for Teachers* of *A Course In Miracles* points out, 'Christ takes many forms with different names until their oneness can be recognized. But Jesus is *for you* the bearer of Christ's single message'.[29]

Readers of the Christian Gospels cannot help reflecting on the saying of Jesus of Nazareth to the effect that 'If anyone says to you then, "Look, here is the Christ", or, "Look, there he is", do not believe it. Impostors will come claiming to be Christs or prophets, and they will produce signs and wonders to mislead, if possible, God's chosen.'[30]

Channelling may be a New Age craze, but it is as ancient as humanity. The idea that men and women could be channels for discarnate wisdom lies at the root of primitive shamanism, the oracular phenomena of ancient Delphi and other sacred places, and the prophecy of the Old Testament. Nor is it far removed from what seems to happen in a great deal of musical, poetic, or literary inspiration.

A shaman, so the Shorter Oxford English Dictionary tells us, is properly the name given to a priest or priest–doctor among the northern Asiatic tribal peoples. The religion of the Ural-Altaic primitives was one in which 'all the good and evil of life are thought to be brought about by spirits which can be influenced only by Shamans'. The term has since been extended to Eskimo and native north-west American peoples, and to tribal religions in the Pacific and elsewhere. Indeed, the phenomenon seems to have been (and still to be) remarkably widespread.[31] But it is not an easy thing to become a shaman:

> You do not become a shaman by initiation or by teaching, or by someone else telling you that you are, or could be, one. You have to have suffered a near-death experience, life-threatening illness or accident during which the inner powers led your dissected body up the Tree of Life and showed you how you would only be healed if you become a shaman and serve your tribe. You would serve the tribe as a healer only by bringing power through from the land of the dead, by entering a deep, near-death trance, seeking the soul of the sick person, and fighting the spirits in the Otherworld to bring it back to life.[32]

This is a far cry from the easy way in which so many modern channellers think they can approach their work. Even after the rigours of shamanic initiation, it is not easy to enter the altered state of consciousness necessary for the work of shamanism. Enforced seclusion, sleep deprivation, and loud and persistent drumming are frequent methods,[33] but psychotropic and dangerous drugs such as fly agaric, mescaline, belladonna, henbane, and ergot have also often featured.[34] How many of us know that the famous hymn by John Greenleaf Whittier, 'Dear Lord and Father of Mankind', was taken from a long poem in which the ancient Hindus were portrayed brewing their *soma* or psychedelic drink?[35] Whittier was showing how different this was from his Quaker experience where, by contrast, the worshippers were reclothed in their rightful mind, to find God's service in purer lives and praise him in deeper reverence.

Drugs apart, there are many similarities between primitive shamans and the prophets of Old Testament times. Johannes Lindblom is particularly effective in drawing them out. He begins his study of Israelite prophecy with a description of Arctic and Ural-Altaic shamans, goes on to talk of the *kahins* and dervishes of the Arab world, and then moves on to other modern parallels in his own Scandinavia. In the light of them he was able to write of the Old Testament prophets that they shared with present-day shamans the

> ability to experience the divine in an original way and to receive revelations from the divine world ... The prophet ... always refers to another who stands behind him and tells him what he

must say ... His thoughts and words never come from himself; they are given him ... Few things are so characteristic of the prophets ... as the feeling of being under a superhuman and supernatural constraint.[36]

After having read the earlier part of this chapter, we may feel that these words of Lindblom's could have been explicitly written about New Age channellers. The only difference seems to be that the prophets of the Old Testament were more under compulsion than the modern channeller. They *had* to prophesy, or else they would have burst. Channellers seem able to decide whether or not to exercise their gift. Once, however, they are actually *in* trance, ancient Israelite prophets and modern channellers are alike when it comes to controlling what they say. Neither of them have any choice. The Old Testament prophets were quite incapable of working to order. Remember the story of Balaam who was hired by Balak to curse the Israelites? Three times over, once he was in prophetic ecstasy, he blessed those he was hired to curse.[37] Or, at any rate, the *true* prophet had no choice. False prophets could pretend to prophesy, but they simply spoke the sort of oracles they were paid to pronounce. So, when four hundred 'prophets' told the king of Israel what he wanted to hear, Jehoshaphat insisted on seeking the oracle from Micaiah, and the true prophet was unable to go with the majority.[38]

The prophets of the Old Testament were channels for the spirit of Jahweh which spoke from within them. They took no responsibility for what they said in their prophetic fit, and they introduced their words with the authority of the stark formula, 'Thus saith Jahweh'. And the succession went on, via the prophets of the New Testament Church[39] and the oracles of John in the Book of Revelation, into later history. The Koran was given to Muhammad in channelled form, and, in the Christian tradition, we go through St Bridget of Sweden,[40] Mother Julian of Norwich with her 'shewings', and a host of others – even Emanuel Swedenborg, and Rudolf Steiner.[41]

Literary, musical, and artistic inspiration is also very akin to channelling. Many a creative genius has said that he was simply a channel for the inspiration which flooded through him, and for which he acted as no more than an amanuensis. Like many others of my generation, I was introduced to parapsychology by reading G. N. M. Tyrrell's Pelican book, *The Personality of Man*. Near the beginning of that book, there is an evocative chapter on the nature of inspiration, largely drawn from an earlier book by Dr Rosamond Harding: 'Those creations of the human mind, which have borne pre-eminently the stamp of originality and greatness ... have come from beyond consciousness, knocking at its door for admittance; they have flowed into it, sometimes slowly as if by seepage, but often with a burst of overwhelming power.'[42] That seems to have been true of inspiration from at least the times of the *daemon* of Socrates, or the voice of which Isaiah speaks when he says that we will hear it from behind us saying, 'This is the way; follow it' (Isa. 30.21). As Lamartine said, 'It is not I who think; it is my thoughts which think for me.'

So channelling is nothing new, and it has parallels with processes which we may not understand, but which are certainly familiar within the norms of our cultural and religious heritage. All very well. But we still have to ask, where does all this channelled or inspired material come from, and can we trust it?

We are not short of hypotheses. There are those who believe, to use the kind of high-flown language beloved of the less reflective of New Age followers, that in it we 'receive, into our current cloud of unknowing, waves of cognition like light streaming from the seat and source of omniscience, omnipotence, and omnipresence'.[43]

According to other commentators, however, the voices may come from less exalted regions. Jungians speak of material which has been obtained by tapping into the Collective Unconscious of the whole human race. There are others who believe that channelling is simply the result of psychological processes which occur when a subject is in an altered state of consciousness. Barbara Honegger (as reported by Jon Klimo)[44] points out that we all have two hemispheres to our brain and that in normal life they work harmoniously together. But, according to her, 'each brain hemisphere has a separate and conscious ego' and 'interhemispheric communication' is possible. In channelling, the *alter ego* of one hemisphere expresses its inner thoughts, desires, and longings to the other. We do not recognize what is happening and we think that we are receiving communications from outside our selves.

Another suggestion comes from Arthur Hastings, who writes that transpersonal psychology 'suggests that there are aspects of the personality, conscious or unconscious, that involve intuition, creativity, purpose and meaning, higher values, transcendent experiences, and spiritual concerns. They are understood to be healthy and a part of human development. It appears that the channeling mode can express or tap into these levels of the self.'[45]

Others suggest that the phenomenon may not be quite as healthy as Hastings makes out. Most people give way at some time or other to a bout of wishful thinking. Some are fantasy-prone; a few are neurotic or even frankly psychotic. The channelling mode may be a self-induced quasi-hypnotic state in which subconsciously-repressed material is let out, using the method of projection, whereby the unresolved part of oneself is presented to consciousness in the guise of an external entity. Many channellers, like many sufferers from multiple personality disorder, have a history of childhood trauma or even abuse. As children they may have coped with persecution by splitting off a sub-personality; as adults, they use the same method to escape the boredom of being ordinary or unnoticed. Most people would like to be 'special', and some of them may compensate for a sense of their own inferiority (or perceived inferiority – 'I'm only a house-wife') by creating a superior being to whom only they have access.

Other commentators on the channelling scene make more serious diagnoses. Perhaps it is the activity of evil and lying spirits intent on our destruction? Jesus the son of Sirach warned us many years ago that 'what the Lord keeps secret is no concern of yours' (Ecclus. 3.22), and it ill behoves us to pry into such matters. That would certainly be the view of most charismatic and conservative Evangelical writers.[46]

Joe Fisher does not fall into either of those latter categories. His cautionary tale is worth our taking note. As an investigative but basically agnostic reporter, he had, earlier, produced books on reincarnation and fortune-telling. He began to look into the channelling phenomenon and was led half-way across the world checking out the details in material he had received in channelled communications. It all proved to be no more than a wild-goose chase. Eventually he concluded that he had been silly to work on the assumption that the material with which he had been presented was worth taking seriously. In the stories the channelling entities were feeding him, there was the occasional grain of truth, but the moment he began serious historical research into them, he discovered that they were almost entirely fictitious, and where they were not, coincidence was a sufficient explanation of the information. He had, he concluded, been the victim of mendacious 'hungry ghosts' who were battening on him and luring him on, because they needed to feed on his vital energy to maintain their own existence.

All these possibilities are not necessarily exclusive. All of them may be true, and what we receive may be an amalgam of material of diverse provenance. Alice Bailey's 'Tibetan' source told her that 'two percent of the material purported to be channeled comes from "masters" to their disciples; 5 percent is from more advanced disciples in training on the inner planes; 8 percent is from the channels' own higher Selves or souls; and some 85 percent is from the personal subconscious of the channels.'[47] No wonder an experienced teacher of channelling, Joey Crinita, reckons that 'most of what novice channels think is channeling is rather the product of self-delusion brought on as a result of psychic immaturity'.[48]

We are left with the main question unresolved. Is channelling genuinely what it purports to be? Or is it the result of a psychological trick which our brains are playing on us? Or is it something much more sinister?

The oldest test is the least reliable: 'When a word spoken by a prophet in the name of the LORD is not fulfilled and does not come true, it is not a word spoken by the LORD. The prophet has spoken presumptuously; have no fear of him' (Deut. 18.22). That is not a great deal of help. Some prophecies take an awful long time to be verified. Others are ambiguous, so that their interpretation will be disputed till the end of time. Much channelled material is not prediction; and even if it were, we know from 2 Corinthians 11.14 that Satan is a past master at disguising himself as an angel of light so that he may mislead the unwary.

Peter Spink asks whether the teaching through the channel promotes dependence and leads to psychological slavery, or whether it allows the recipient to advance towards a greater growth into spiritual maturity and a fuller realization of his own human potential.[49] If the latter, then he is prepared to allow that the channelled material is worth following. That is an improvement on the Deuteronomist's view, and certainly coheres with what Joe Fisher discovered during his exploration into the channelling world; but it still does not go far enough. Teaching, for all it emphasizes human potential, could still be plain wrong. What is meant by 'spiritual maturity'? It is differently conceived by different teachers. We need some criteria to help us decide.

The first letter of John (1 John 4.1) does not tell us to reject every spirit. It tells us to test them, to see whether they acknowledge Jesus as the incarnate Christ. On that test, not much channelled material would qualify. April Radbill, on behalf of the Research Committee of Spiritual Frontiers Fellowship International, has analysed 'What Spirit Communicators say about God'. In the channelled material at which she has looked, God is described as 'a great life force, undifferentiated or unintentioned or specialized, a spiritual blood stream'. Or, again, 'God is an aware intelligence whose components are individual people who live and think as individuals, from the time of their origin until and including their return to the Godhead of All-Knowingness'. And there is much more along similar lines. It does not bear much resemblance to what Christian theologians have said about God over the ages.

In the end we come down to the business of spiritual discernment, where there are no rules, but what we seek is enough wisdom to guide us on our way. 'Sources' which spew out stereotypical psycho-babble by the bucketful, or give us an optimistic superfluity of the kind of moral uplift which we would have been capable of writing for ourselves, do not do anybody any real good. They give us no help whatever to face the inner darkness against which each of us will come at some stage in the course of our pilgrimage here on earth. They have no conception of what is meant by the 'dark night', whether of soul or spirit.

Christians are moral, but they place morality in a wider context. Exhortations to be kind and think good thoughts are compatible with Christianity, but they are not in themselves evidence of a Christian content to the communication, not even when (perhaps especially not even when) they are conjoined with dire warnings about the eternal consequences of not listening to them. For real discernment we need a metaphysical and theological overview. We need a system of thought within which to place the ideas we receive and whereby we may judge which of them we should assimilate and which reject. And – in the end – it is by their fruits that we shall know them; the fruits not only of individual lives which are either enhanced or drained by being channels or by heeding material which comes via channels, but the fruits of a vision for society and nations.

That leads us once more to the difference between an eclectic New Age philosophy and the doctrine of the Christian Church. It is time for us to draw the threads of our whole investigation together, and to see what the New Age as a totality has to say to the Church, and what the Church has to say to New Agers as the third Christian millennium approaches.

11
Christian Reactions

What are Christians to make of all this? As usual, there is a very wide range of possible options.

1.

Some Christians believe that New Age ideas are insidious and dangerous, and that the best form of defence against them is attack. They react, therefore, by loud denunciations of everything which might be associated with New Age ideas. An over-interest in Green issues is particularly suspect. One such commentator writes that 'we could imagine, for example, a teacher becoming enthusiastic about environmental issues and taking a party of children to Findhorn'. (Findhorn lies about 120 miles north of Edinburgh, so the scenario is a little unlikely, but we will let that pass.) He continues:

> Such a vist for some children could be the beginning of a series of steps leading into all that New Age and occult can bring forth ... Perhaps the warning signals should sound for us when we see non-Christian organizations campaigning for radical change, or promoting global plans. We must remember that any such wide-ranging scheme will involve people with a wide spectrum of religious beliefs. Thus, when a spiritual dimension becomes part of that global plan it is bound to have some sort of multi-faith expression, and this provides a doorway for New Age ideas.[1]

On this view, since the New Age dislikes dogmatism, Christian dogmatists need to react by stressing their distinctive doctrines all the more insistently. That may, of course, repel those who are attracted by New Age ideas, and will confirm their suspicion that the Christian Church is not for them. It is a risk worth taking. We shall have pointed unequivocally to Christian truths and maintained the integrity of the Faith which has been under attack. And who knows? The New Ager may see the error of his ways, and we shall then have made a convert.

So, they say, we need to be on the watch against anything that smacks of compromise. One of our targets will be the ecologists and anybody who believes that, in the face of threats to the environment and the living globe, there should be attempts to find common ground between adherents of the different faiths. An Evangelical Alliance pamphlet *New Age Promise: Age Old Problem?* warns us that

> Political movements, particularly the Greens in Germany, ask for the political implementation of New Age goals. While a group called Planetary Citizens, who are 'dedicated to the transformation of the world through political action', includes many notable New Agers and occultists among its leaders. It was founded by a consultant to the United Nations.

The World Wide Fund for Nature and the International Consultancy on Religion, Education, and Culture are especial targets for this kind of attack because they have sponsored inter-faith events with an ecological thrust. So we are warned that 'the danger with Harvest Festivals always was that they would glorify the creation and man, not God Himself',[2] and this danger was not avoided in the numerous Creation-Centred Liturgies in the late 1980s and early 1990s. At a Coventry Cathedral celebration, for example, 'the service ended with a New Age ceremony ... The tree, "the conservationist's symbol of life", [was] presented by the Director of WWF-UK to the Provost.'[3]

It is in this spirit that a pamphlet on New Age Networks and Extensions can warn its readers of links which could 'take people from a peripheral activity into the main New Age network'. The writer includes 'Cathedrals', the 'Ecumenical Movement', and 'Mystical and Heretical Christians' (naming Teilhard de Chardin as an example) in a diagram of 'Extensions to the New Age Network'.[4] Another writer[5] states quite categorically that the Campaign for Nuclear Disarmament is part of the New Age movement.

All this seems to me to have fallen into the trap of overestimating both the power and the ubiquity of New Age thinking, and of undiscriminatingly tarring with the New Age brush everything which does not accord with its own perception of acceptably Christian thought and behaviour.

The same is true of the 'conspiracy theory'. This takes the wilder utterances of some writers associated with New Age thinking as evidence that there is a secret plan to take over the whole world and forcibly convert it to New Age ideas. We are warned that 'A worldwide network of many thousands of co-operating organizations, the New Age Movement aims primarily at the formation of a "New World Order" marked by "group consciousness" and "synergy" (combined activity).'[6] The same writer claims that the secret teachings of Alice Bailey 'are followed minutely in New Age circles',[7] and that 'the main political goal of the New Age movement is global control'.[8] Dr Margaret Brearley, Senior Fellow at the Centre for Judaism of the Selly Oak Colleges at Birmingham, sees a real danger in the fact that the New Age is a neo-pagan, neo-fascist movement which would like to (and conceivably could) destroy Christianity and Judaism in a new Holocaust, as the Nazis tried to do in Third Reich Germany. Included in the teachings of the New Age movement, according to a leaflet put out by Upper Room Tracts of Great Yarmouth, are 'forced redistribution of world resources through a "World Food Authority"' and 'A new world religion – World Council of Churches'.

It is hard to resist the conclusion that the real aim of the more florid of these accusations is to be like the Fat Boy in *Pickwick Papers*, who used to come up to unsuspecting old ladies and say, 'I wants to make your flesh creep'. They would like people to believe that the system of which they so strongly disapprove is potentially a great deal more powerful than appears on the surface. If they can frighten enough people with their stories about its plans, folk will see how important it is not to give such dangerous ideas even the slightest of footholds. 'The world is an appallingly bad place', they say, 'and you will be amazed at the kinds of wickedness we are uncovering about it. It clearly isn't safe for you to be around, unless, of course, you stick with us, in which case you will be all right.'

People who fear the New Age because they believe the conspiracy theory seem to have taken Marilyn Ferguson's title *The Aquarian Conspiracy* too literally. What she was describing was a movement of thought which was so widespread that people who espoused it were surprised to discover how many people in their chosen field or their organization shared their ideas, so that they felt like conspirators when they shared their 'heretical' insights with each other. Admittedly, there are sections in the voluminous writings of Alice Bailey which sound as though she would have welcomed the chance of world domination, but they are not likely to spark off a bloody revolution in which the Old Agers will be put to the sword by those who espouse the new ideas (a scenario which Randall Baer seems to find believable). The New Age movement is just not that kind of animal.

Michael Cole sets forth the pros and cons of accepting the conspiracy theory and seems to be unpersuaded of it.[9] He ends, however, by hedging his bets. It is impossible to settle the matter, he concludes, but certainly the New Age movement is the ground for a 'power encounter' between Satan and God.

For an excellent critique of the conspiracy theory, of which the most notable protagonist is Constance Cumbey in her book, *The Hidden Dangers of the Rainbow*, see the analysis of over forty titles by James R. Lewis in *The New Age Movement: A Bibliography of Conservative Christian Literature*.

Christian traducers of the New Age movement can sometimes make very odd speculations about it. An editorial in the magazine *Prophecy Today*[10] suggested that some followers of witchcraft had been working by occult means to undermine family life and marriage, especially among Christians (that does not seem to comport very well with 'an ye harm none, do what ye will'). It then went on to speculate that the discovery of a blackbird hanging from an oak tree a mile or two from the East Midlands airport was 'clear evidence of witchcraft activity' and that this activity may well have caused the confusion in the mind of the pilot which led to the Kegworth disaster of January 1989. I suppose it is just possible that telepathic activity could have confused the pilot's thought processes, though it seems an unlikely hypothesis. But to link a dead blackbird with witchcraft (when Wicca explicitly renounces any practice of sacrifice) shows a complete misunderstanding of that Craft. Farm labourers might put a dead bird on a twig as a scarecrow device, or sick-minded characters might treat small creatures as flies to wanton boys, but to credit such people with wide-ranging psychic powers is unlikely in the extreme, and it certainly has nothing to do either with witchcraft or the New Age.

This whole approach is specifically designed to draw sharp lines between what its proponents regard as authentic Christianity and anything which can be remotely construed as having anything to do with New Age. Its purpose is to warn the faithful lest they be compromised, and to maintain the purity of faith as defined by a group that feels threatened by any kind of infiltration that might reduce its power over its followers. This approach sees Christianity and the New Age as diametrically opposed, and insists that it is not possible to serve two such incompatible masters.

2.

This, however, is not the only way for Christians. Some of them take a much more positive and affirmative view of New Age concerns.

As we have already seen, St James's Church in Piccadilly has been well known in this respect for the last decade or more, ever since Donald Reeves became its rector. His view is that the church needs to provide a place where it can show its repentance for the unfriendly way in which it has treated people who are on a genuine and profoundly serious spiritual search. New Agers are not prepared to accept a pre-packaged and dogmatically-defined version of Christianity, but if we are more relaxed towards each other, there are plenty of insights we can share. Indeed, each can learn from the other in the process.

One way in which this is expressed at St James's is through its 'Creation-centred Spirituality' group. Members take many of their insights from the writings of Matthew Fox. Although this group is Christian in intention, its Christianity is a remarkably eclectic version of the Faith. For example, it finds much which is of value in the pre-Christian Celtic pagan religion of this land as well as in the insights of the Celtic Christian saints like Cuthbert and Aidan. We have already remarked on the way in which native American spirituality can act as an Old Testament on transatlantic soil. In an exactly parallel way, Britain's native Celtic traditions are seen by 'Creation-centred Spirituality' as a *praeparatio evangelica*. So 'we find joy and kinship with each other, with Mother Earth, and with the whole cosmos'. This ecumenism is experienced as being much deeper than the ecclesially-centred ecumenism of Councils of Churches, and is closer to an inter-faith dialogue than to a domestically Christian concern.

But it is in 'Alternatives' that St James's Church and the New Age movement come closest together. This is the name given to a programme directed by Dr William Bloom and others, and hosted by the church. The 'friendly disclaimer' on the Alternatives programme explains that although St James's, in its generosity and openness of mind, hosts Alternatives, the ideas in its programme are not representative of St James's itself.

Alternatives makes no bones about being a totally New Age programme, without recognizably or specifically Christian input. In the summer of 1991, it included lectures on 'Electro-Crystal Therapy', 'Evil, Karma and Grace', and a Summer Solstice Celebration 'in honour of the passing of the seasons, in honour of the Sun'.

On one of those evenings, I was present when Joy Balles-Beeson was addressing the gathering. We came across her channelling activity in our previous chapter. She was also expounding the techniques of 'Psychological-Kinesiology'. Explaining how we all carry around with us the hurts of several past lifetimes, she expounded a technique of body posture and muscle control which, so she claimed, would help us gain access to our hidden emotions, de-stress us, and remove the blocks which were preventing our higher self from being effective in our lives. There was mention of the need for psychic protection, but no mention of God or of Jesus during the whole evening.

Alternatives meets in the church building itself, sweet with the gentle odour of burning joss-sticks. Its lectures can attract crowds of a couple of hundred or more on a Monday evening. Some of the audience will be 'regulars', others have come either because they are particularly interested in the evening's subject or speaker or because, as Christians or New Agers or interested outsiders, they want to see how two such apparently diverse communities as the Church and the New Age can co-exist.

It seems, however, to be co-existence rather than dialogue. The 'arm's length' policy which St James's Church operates towards Alternatives means there is no meeting of minds between them on a Monday evening. I would, of course, guess that there is a great deal of questioning and discussion going on between participants, audience, and others as a result of it; but Alternatives itself is organized and presented as frankly and completely New Age without any Christian veneer. The brochure says that

> Alternatives of St James's is dedicated to New Age thinking: ideas which provide creative and spiritual alternatives to currently accepted Western thought. Our purpose is to provide a friendly atmosphere in which to taste the best of New Age ideas. We are dedicated to the freedom of each individual to choose her or his own path of personal and spiritual growth.

Certainly there is no patronizing Christian condescension behind the scenes here. Anything of that kind would be immediately detected and disavowed.

It is for the experiencer to make up her or his own mind as to what is inferred by the hosting of such a programme by a Christian church. Is it an exercise in incompatibility or do the two communities have things to learn from each other?

The claim of this experiment would be that any Christian ministry to the New Age which is any more high-profile than Alternatives would be counter-productive, and that there are better ways of winning people for Christ than to try to argue with them. The point can be made by quoting Christians who are far from New Age enthusiasts. It may be illustrated from an Eastertide sermon I heard preached in Durham Cathedral by the Dean, John Arnold. He was speaking about the incident in Luke 24, when two disciples walking to Emmaus were met on the road by a stranger. He kept company with them for several miles and opened their eyes to many things in the Scriptures whose significance had previously escaped them. Understanding, said the Dean, comes by walking alongside someone on the road and facing in the same direction as him. Truth is rarely discovered when we face each other in the confrontational way beloved of media presenters.

Well and good; the principle of walking beside the New Ager rather than firing shots at him is a good one. There is, however, as always, a danger in taking a good principle too far. In the St James's case, the danger is that the Church will be playing host to ideas which are incompatible with even the most liberal theology. Hence there arise misunderstandings and recriminations. It is a bold step, instead of attacking New Agers, to invite them to come in and to take your premises over for a while. But will what is taken over be not only the physical building for an evening a week, but also the witness of that building to a gospel which it was placed there, and maintained over the centuries, to proclaim? And will outsiders be given the wrong message about what it is that the Church exists for and teaches? The authorities at St James's do not seem to think so; but the questions nag, and unease is not entirely quieted.

3.

Canon Peter Spink's method of engagement with New Age ideas is different again, though it has much in common with the convictions which lie behind what is going on at St James's.

Winford Priory, now the home of the Omega Order which he founded in 1980, is a beautifully restored eighteenth-century house in the heart of the countryside, a few miles south of Bristol. The peace is almost palpable, as one enters into the common room to be faced by a bronzed cast of St Benedict, holding a copy of the Holy

Rule which Benedict himself modestly described as a little rule for beginners who love life and would see good days.

It could have been any retreat house or monastic community, apart perhaps from one or two large pictures of a mystical character which were on loan and being exhibited whilst I was there, emphasizing that the veil between the physical world and that which lies beyond is a great deal more diaphanous than many people would acknowledge. (It is also, incidentally, the only community house I know which sells colour postcards of the Prior and his dog, but that's another matter.) And the choice of reading matter is more eclectic than the casual visitor might have expected.

The patron saints of Winford Priory include Pierre Teilhard de Chardin and F. C. Happold, a schoolmaster who died in the 1950s and who wrote a number of books on Christian mysticism. As in many a Christian house, the heart of the day is the eucharistic liturgy. Here it is introduced with fine classical music and interspersed with contemplative dance, and the central Prayer of Thanksgiving is especially composed by the Order and spoken by everybody present.

On one of the days when I was there, the scriptural reading reminded us that it was by faith that Abraham, though he dwelt in the land of promise, lived in it as in a foreign country (Heb. 11.9). The Omega Order witnesses to the truth that we are heirs to that promise, whose fulfilment came many generations later than Abraham; and so we can live in the land of promise as citizens rather than as aliens. Thus there is less of a sense of spiritual warfare and more of a sense of laying hold of God's promises. We can therefore receive the deep peace of the running wave, the deep peace of the flowing air, the deep peace of the quiet earth and the shining stars, and, above all, the deep peace of the Son of the God of all creation who is the Prince of Peace, and who dwells in the hearts of all who love him.

Peter Spink first heard of the New Age about twenty years ago at a Wrekin Trust conference on Iona addressed by Sir George Trevelyan. He was so impressed that he began from then to follow a way which recognized that the God of the mystics was a more inclusive God than the God of the dogmaticians, and that there were many people for whom that kind of God was a great deal more congenial. One of the aims of the Omega Order is 'to recognize Christ under all forms to the exclusion of none', and therefore to welcome folk of all religions (or even of none) so long as they are seriously seeking for truth.

Peter Spink has written a number of books in which he explores the boundaries between New Age thought and Christian doctrine. The New Age, he points out, is 'non-dogmatic and has to do with a higher level of consciousness where the truth is seen, not as a set of intellectual definitions but rather as that which awakens to reality'.[11] But then, in Christianity also, 'doctrines and formularies ... do not themselves constitute the truth. They are simply a means of its expression ... The Gospel of Jesus Christ will, if we refuse to imprison it within a set of intellectual propositions, be seen and heard to speak directly and powerfully to today's widespread quest for truth.'[12] It is in the mystical awareness that all religions begin to find a unity deeper than their doctrinal differences. This is what Aldous Huxley, in his book with that title, called the 'Perennial Philosophy': 'At the heart of each religion, without exception, was a tradition and practice of spirituality resulting in sheer goodness where all were essentially one ... [This was] an essential unity regardless of differing and often diametrically opposed belief patterns.'[13]

In the light of that approach, Peter Spink claims to have found much that he wishes to affirm within New Age teachings. The starting-point of his enquiry was not God, but the human being. It was about human beings that people were asking questions, and 'the clergy are past masters at the art of answering questions that nobody is asking'.[14] We cannot win people by asking them to submit to external authority or dogma, but only on the basis of knowledge gained through experience. That is why the exploration of the inner worlds undertaken by such people as Annie Besant and Rudolf Steiner with their Theosophical and Anthroposophical teaching is so important to him.[15] Christians may reject this as Gnostic and scientists as something inherently unverifiable; but to Peter Spink it is the possibility of a leap forward towards spiritual maturity. It leads us to the still centre at the heart of our being. We should not see ourselves as guilty selves before a wrathful deity. Our aim is not self-denial so much as self-realization. There is a movement towards human fulfilment and humanity's true destiny, and Christians and New Agers alike can share in it: 'A new and universal self-awareness is struggling to be born. Its distinctive characteristic is a realization of a unity which, existing already at a deeper level, is now seeking to manifest at all levels of society.'[16]

This means that we ought not to be so concerned with the presence of evil as we so often are. We are not required to believe in evil, to concede to it the substance of reality. To believe in evil is to confer existence upon it. If we refuse to give evil any right to existence, it will be nullified and its operations quelled.[17] We should keep our thoughts on what is true, pure and of good report, because 'this Christ principle may be defined as ... the highest of all energies, that of love. This energy is seeking to manifest itself at all levels of creation through a process of evolution.'[18]

So the Omega Order was founded in order to recover a sense of a unity in contemplative and mystical awareness which could transcend, not only differences between Christians, but differences between people of other religions as well. The Order numbers amongst its members Roman Catholic and Anglican priests as well as lay people, both single and married. It seeks to speak especially to those who have been damaged by that kind of insensitive teaching which has repressed their true selves in the interests of a spurious spirituality.

That is one reason why a particular emphasis at Winford is the teaching of the Enneagram, done by the Sub-Prior, a Roman Catholic layman by the name of James Fahey. The Enneagram[19] is a personality inventory, though a more ancient one than that of Myers and Briggs which is currently so popular. It can act as a map of redemption and a way towards self-knowledge. Pre-Christian in origin, it has been honed and perfected by Sufi mystics and American Jesuits until it has come to its present form.

The basic premise of the Enneagram is that all humans are made in the perfect image of God, but that all of us have distorted that image, each in her or his own individual way. Only so have we been able to cope with the world and its demands as we have discovered them in early childhood. Each of us fits into one or other of nine personality types. We are usually ready enough to acknowledge that much; most of us, however, are largely unaware of the shadow side of each of the types, and of how important this has been in our own personal pilgrimage through life. By means of the Enneagram we can look at our self without guilt, discover our true giftedness as God-given, and thereby be enabled to open to life more fully, live more freely, and look to God directly for healing or redemption.

That kind of self-affirmation in God's eyes does not come easily to Englishmen who have been taught, from the cradle upwards, to be self-deprecating. But only if we are at harmony with ourselves as well as at harmony with the outside world (the physical world as well as the world of our fellow-humans) can we hope to enjoy that

harmony with God our Creator and Redeemer which is his wish
for us.

In ways like this, many of the needs which have been expressed by
the New Age movement are being addressed at Winford Priory,
within a relaxed and Christian context and in the silence of contemplation. The gospel thereby is enabled to liberate those who had
feared that it was going to be merely something negative and
repressive.

There are blind spots in this approach. It would not do for the
whole of the Christian Church to be satisfied with a non-dogmatic
mysticism which regarded the differentia between itself and other
faiths as of little concern. Sin and evil are seriously underestimated.
If the cross and atonement ever became as peripheral to Christianity
as they appear to be in Peter Spink's published writings, something
would be seriously wrong. It could also be alleged (with selective
quotations to make the point) that, in the thinking behind the
Omega Order, human needs are more determinative than the
exploration of the divine nature.

But that is not the real point. If we imagined we could ever find a
single congregation, or a single religious order, which expressed the
whole of Christian truth in perfect proportion and harmony, we
would soon find out that we were looking for a manifest impossibility.
So we ought not to damn the Omega Order for not expressing some
things about Christianity which *we* feel to be important, or
for accepting ideas which we feel are inconsistent with our understanding of the faith or mutually incompatible with each other. All of
us sin in that way to some extent, and none of us is qualified to cast
the first stone. What is of much greater significance is that there are
people around who have been damaged by their exposure to a
version of Christianity which has repressed them rather than affirmed
their basic human value, or which has denied insights into the nature
of reality which they feel to be valid. For them, the experience of an
accepting community such as the Omega Order can be an important
way into saving faith. There is room within Christianity for such an
order, and we should be glad that it exists, even if we find there are
things about it with which we might wish to disagree.

4.

That is not the end of our discussion about Christian ways of
reacting to the New Age. If we are neither fundamentalists nor

members of St James's Piccadilly, nor Companions of the Omega Order, but still want to think about Christianity in the light of New Age concerns, what particular aspects of Christian doctrine ought we to be exploring? An evangelical writer recently commented:

> The new paradigm posited by the New Age *may* [my italics] be a neutral phenomenon to which erroneous theological ideas and spiritual practices can become attached, as to any other culture. In that case it would be incumbent on Christians to produce their own spirituality and theology for the New Age ... Just as cultural pressures led to the reformulation of Christology in relation to new questions at the Council of Nicaea, so we are being forced to reformulate the Christian faith in relation to new questions.[20]

There needs to be dialogue between Christians and New Agers, so that each may the better understand the other. This has already begun. One such attempt was held at Findhorn in November 1990. Sadly, however, it looked from the report of the conference[21] as if there was very little serious theological input. It characterized the essential message of Christianity as 'Love, Peace, and Justice'. Love, peace, and justice are desperately important, but they do not define Christianity. I was reminded of the description an American friend once gave me of New England Unitarianism: 'It is all about the Fatherhood of God, the Brotherhood of Man, and the Neighbourhood of Boston'.

The report seemed to conclude that it was the Christians who needed to make all the adjustments, and that New Age ideas were beyond criticism. Thus, it drew attention to the paradigm shift within twentieth-century Christianity that has resulted in a greater degree of ecumenical understanding between separated Christians. The paradigm shift of the twenty-first century, it went on, needs to be towards the 'deeper ecumenism' of inter-faith convergence. That simply will not do. If that were to be the solution, it would simply mean assimilating Christianity to New Age ideas and turning it into an emasculated and undistinctive faith which would be as syncretistic, eclectic, and undogmatic as the New Age itself, married (as Dean Inge once said) to the spirit of this age and therefore likely to be a widow in the next.

If that is not good enough, what moves ought we to be making towards mutual understanding? We must not compromise the integrity of the Christian faith, but new occasions teach new duties, and new questions bring new understandings out of old doctrines. If Christianity is to appeal to those who have rejected it in favour of New Age teaching, we need to see whether what they have rejected is true Christianity or a parody of true Christianity, or whether their very rejection is a sign to us that our own understanding of Christianity is in need of revision. Those are questions which we need to explore in our final chapter.

12

The Stigma
of Dogma

In the last few chapters, we have looked at particular manifestations of New Age practices and examined a mass of detail. It is time now to stand back from the detail and concentrate once more on the basic underlying ideas of the New Age movement. Behind all the dazzle of what Carol Riddell of Findhorn dismisses as 'a large coterie of "psychic entrepreneurs" who advertise their wares in the host of "new age" magazines',[1] and the 'endless wanderings in the labyrinthine ways of psychic culs-de-sac' against which Peter Spink warns us,[2] there lies a genuine disenchantment with the cruder aspects of late twentieth-century materialism, and a real spiritual search.

Three ideas in particular recur in many New Age systems. Can we look at them once more in the light of what we now know about the New Age as a whole, and hear what they are saying to the Christian Church as it enters its third millennium? As we do so, we will be repeating some material from earlier chapters, but in a wider context than we did the first time round. The three basic convictions are that:

1. Civilization in the twentieth-century West has taken a wrong turning, from which mankind and the eco-system of the earth need to be rescued.
2. A transformative human experience can restore meaning to our lives.
3. We can have spirituality without dogma if we penetrate to the mystical, unifying, core at the centre of all religion.

1. There is wide disenchantment with the way in which the technological advances of the present century have been bought at the price of the dehumanization of society and the pillage of nature. The twentieth century has been an age of wars and rumours of wars, and there is a widespread weariness with the futility of it all. Not

many people will see the passing of the century of the world wars and Hiroshima, of lost forests and punctured ozone layers, of pollution and famine, with much regret. Can the next century be any better?

Perhaps it can. The slogan that 'small is beautiful' finds echoes in many a heart, and Green movements are growing in numbers and influence. Can they succeed in rescuing humanity from its suicidal madness? Yes, say New Agers; because the universe itself is on our side. We are about to enter the Age of Aquarius. Astrology confirms our feeling that we are at one of the fulcrums of history, and that things in the coming age are going to be very different. Maybe it really is true, as the Christmas carol assures us, that

> ... the days are hastening on,
> By prophet bards foretold,
> When, with the ever circling years
> Comes round the age of gold.[3]

There is a paradox here. We are at the dawn of a new astrological age, and change therefore *must* come about. But the New Age is the Age of Aquarius, the water-carrier who is going to pour the freedom of the spirit over the whole earth. This means that change must come through freedom rather than compulsion. We are not in the grip of an inexorable Fate. Astrology is about constraints and opportunities, not about letting the inevitable take its course. If we seize our opportunities, the universe will co-operate. A new, spiritualized, age is on its way. The tide has turned. If enough people co-operate, the earth and the people on it may be saved. There is hope; but it needs effort.

The effort will be misplaced if it is an effort to continue in the old ways. The wrong turning which we took was not only a wrong turning towards science and technology; it was a wrong turning away from the ancient spiritual wisdom of an earlier age which was closer to nature and may therefore have been closer to spiritual truth. (That conviction has an affinity with the eighteenth-century romantic idea of the 'noble savage' whom some philosophers of that age believed would be found in the newly discovered islands of the southern Pacific.)

New Agers therefore look for a lost wisdom – the wisdom of one of the ancient Eastern religions (often in a modernized and Westernized form), or the wisdom of the old pagan religion of these islands, or of the native Amerindian culture, or of the Qabalah, or of a supposed civilization of the lost continent of Atlantis, or even an ancient wisdom which has existed in other worlds or on other planes or at other 'vibrations', and is being channelled to earth by benign and superior beings.

Yet, paradoxically, this appeal to an ancient lost wisdom is often buttressed by references to the latest scientific theorizing. Heisenberg's Uncertainty Principle, holography, and Chaos Theory frequently feature in the New Age apologia. They may not be understood, but they have a powerful appeal. It is all part of the feeling that, as a New Age is coming, there will be a new science to support it. Deterministic science led in the twentieth century to the ills from which we are now suffering. A new understanding of the natural world, in which the experimenter is a necessary part of his experiment, and his attitude affects his results, will assist in the birth of an age which is more humane and more spiritual. Science can no longer support an appeal to determinism; the freedom of the Aquarian spirit will be scientifically respectable in the Aquarian Age.

2. The New Age quest is a search for a transformative human experience. There are several steps along the way towards it. The first is to seek freedom from guilt-inducing, self-denying, hierarchical, institutional, dogmatic, anathematizing, authoritarian religions like Christianity. We need, say New Agers, to break free from the conditioning of our early years. When we were tiny children, we thought we were at the centre of the universe and that everything in it existed simply to serve us. Our parents had to oversee the move from this infantile perception of the universe to one in which we saw ourselves as part of a much wider system in which we had to co-exist with a host of other selves, each of them with needs as great as our own. Sadly, they often did this by saddling us with an inner 'parent' who hung round our necks like the Ancient Mariner's albatross and who kept on telling us that we were without ultimate worth or value. That inner parent is still with so many of us, and we have therefore never achieved the potential that should be ours as human beings.

There is a parody of Christian teaching which is often encountered in New Age circles. Christians, they say, believe that all human beings (themselves included) are worthless sinners. To be a good Christian, you have to be full of the guilt which is inseparable from the very fact of being human. You will, however, be all right if you keep reminding your God how basically unworthy you are. If you

143

do this well enough, God may love you enough to allow you to go to heaven, where you can spend an eternity glorifying God by disparaging yourself.

Unfortunately, this attitude is exactly what some Christian priests and parents have succeeded in inducing in their children or charges. Brian Thorne gives some horrifying examples of what can happen. He was once, he tells us, at an international conference in Paris where participants began to talk about their early experiences:

> There was the man brought up in a Catholic boarding school, where the staff – mostly priests – inflicted a vicious round of humiliating punishments for the smallest misdemeanours ... There was the account of a Calvinist minister who had told a fifteen year old that she was possessed by the devil and should on no account enter a chapel building. The stories were not only of priests, nuns and ministers but also of parents whose religious beliefs and practices seemed to make it impossible for them to relate to their children without at the same time judging them, condemning them and making them feel so burdened with guilt that life was almost intolerable.[4]

The seminar was saved from being a complete nightmare by the story of a woman who had, as a young girl, been counselled by a wise Jesuit priest whose name – she later learned – was Fr Pierre Teilhard de Chardin.

Brian Thorne is a Christian psychotherapist and can recognize bad religion when he sees it. The bad kind of religion enables some Christians to build up a mental picture of a male and vengeful God, who can (for example) try to smack down a questioning bishop by setting on fire the cathedral in which he was consecrated. Nonsense of that sort is still at large, and it is responsible for much of the distrust of Christianity by New Agers. Dr Serena Roney-Dougal tells how the nuns at her convent school taught her that there was a link between Eve and evil,[5] so that, until she shook off the effects of this early conditioning, she grew up believing that she was tainted by the very fact of being female.

It will take a lot of patient teaching, over a long period of time, to exorcise that kind of wickedness. We can *say* that the Christian faith is that each individual is a child of God and is of such infinite value in God's eyes that God is willing to die for her; but it will cut little ice with those whose lives have been spoilt by a sadism as vicious as the examples we have just cited, or who see a Church in which a high proportion of its members want to deny full rights to that half of the human race from which the larger proportion of its congregations is drawn.

As Denis Nineham has recently remarked, in reviewing a book on the Catholic Church and sexuality, 'The Church has very little to be proud of in its attitude to women and to sex; and it will have still less to be proud of if it attempts to use past attitudes to the matter to control present attitudes.'[6]

The Hebraic prohibition of graven images, conjoined with the Christian mistrust of the body and its sexuality, has been a major contributor to the rise of pornography. Any visitor to the National Museum in Athens, seeing the way in which the ancient Greeks glorified in the human form, can be forgiven for wondering whether the Judaeo-Christian tradition in this regard has not been a bad mistake from which our contemporary culture is still suffering.

In place of this, New Agers seek a system which will affirm the value of the human being, and – especially – of the human female. They hope that a process of self-knowledge and inner exploration will lead to the discovery of a suitable transformative technique whereby human potential can be realized, and we can discover the gods within us.

There are many such techniques, and we have been introduced to some of them in the pages of this book. They are on offer at such jamborees as the Festival of Mind/Body/Spirit or through the pages of New Age magazines. They range from channelling and past-life therapy to rebirthing or the interpretation of the near-death experience. Many of them are variations on very ancient techniques, but, as we have seen, their antiquity is a positive virtue to the seeker who wishes to turn his back on an unhappy familiarity with contemporary society. It is common for a seeker to be on a continual transformative process, succeeding with technique after technique, but never permanently settling with one. Presumably the 'high' that is achieved when the transformation occurs is a little like an addictive drug.

The experience of 'inner transformation' reads very like an account of a religious conversion. But the conversion is usually to an inner conviction of the value of the self, rather than to a realization of a transcendent Other. Werner Erhard, for instance, has written (my italics) that 'What happened had no form. It was timeless, unbounded, ineffable, beyond language ... I realized that I knew everything ... I was whole and complete as I was, and now I could accept the whole truth about myself. *For I was its source.*[7] An advertisement for a series of cassettes of channelled material promises that 'these cassettes are designed for your personal growth. In a deeply relaxed and creative way you will clear out negative patterns, develop communication with Higher Self and attain higher levels of consciousness.'

This leads, therefore, to an affirmation of the value of the human person. At its most extreme, it can be expressed in the words made famous by the New Age writer and film star Shirley MacLaine: 'I am God. You are God. Everyone is God. Everyone.' If (according to popular New Age theology) there is no external transcendent God, but everything that is, is part of God, then obviously there are gods within every human being. The statement, however, is empty of all meaning, since it could be spoken equally well of a flower, a flea, or a piece of rock. But that kind of deduction is not usually made, and the statement is taken as being a declaration about human potential. It can lead to 'a mystical consciousness or awareness, frequently called by such names as higher consciousness, self-realization, Christ consciousness or New Age awareness.'[8]

This transformation and its concomitant affirmation give the believer a faith in himself which can help him enormously in his work. The typical New Ager is not like the typical 1960s hippie. He is well dressed, he cares for his health, and he is disciplined. He knows how to succeed in his work. He is a product of the post-Reagan, post-Thatcher age. There is an alliance between capitalism and spirituality; there can be 'angels in pinstripes'. Success in life is an indication that the spiritual teaching about self-worth and self-fulfilment is working. There is plenty of use of New-Age-based technique in business training, and no sense that there is an inherent contradiction in harnessing New Age ideas to the needs of the acquisitive society. Indeed, to some extent, people only feel the need for a New Age type of spirituality if they are materially successful yet feel that, despite their affluence, the inner meaning of life has somehow passed them by.[9]

The other side of this kind of affirmation is that there is little room for the unaffirming, the depressive, the unsuccessful, in a New Age community. Carol Riddell, writing about Findhorn, lets this particular cat out of the bag when she says that 'every now and again, a member loses their inspiration for living here ... Then the Personnel Department enters into a gentle process of negotiation, to see if the Foundation is really the place for that person to stay. Signs of inappropriateness might be ... a lack of vibrancy in day-to-day life.'[10]

3. A third characteristic of New Age is a distrust of dogma and a belief that we need to find the mystical core which lies at the centre of all religions. In our increasingly multicultural society, we are becoming more and more aware of the variety of religions, and less and less inclined to be absolutist about any one of them. The New Age takes this tendency to its logical conclusion, and treats belief as a matter, not of discovering the truth, but of following one's personal preference. Beliefs are malleable and subordinate to experience. 'In today's world', writes Carol Riddell,

> the parochial belief that there is only one 'true' religion, whose job is to take over all the others, finally has to be abandoned. If God is the Indweller, the reality in us all, then how we seek to discover Him is a matter of cultural background, of personal choice. Our job is to find that means of Self-discovery that best leads us forward from our present starting point.[11]

Within the New Age, there is no imposed orthodoxy, and 'dogma' is a dirty word. As the old saw had it, a stigma is what you use to beat down a dogma. Any old stigma will do, so long as it drives the dogma away.

Thus, when he was lecturing at the Festival of Mind/Body/Spirit,[12] Sir George Trevelyan spoke a good deal of theology, and obviously was drawing on a great bank of doctrine; but he was insistent that dogma was one of the curses of religion. He resolved the paradox, in true New Age fashion, by saying, in effect, 'This is what things look like to me. If it doesn't seem like that to you, you don't have to accept what I say. Only accept what rings true to your own Inner Self.'

The New Age conception of God, therefore, is very different from the Christian. There is a basic and universal spiritual energy, but this is not the personal God of Christianity. We may call it what we will: 'One may talk of the Indweller as "God", "Jehovah", "Allah", the "Atman", the "Essence", the "Oneness behind all diversity", or "the Christ consciousness". What we find does not differ; the various names and forms in worship are labels and practices to help us'.[13]

Though we may call God what we will, some names are discouraged in a New Age context. This is particularly true of the title 'Father', which is perceived as being sexist, and as throwing us back to the concept of an angry God who is always wanting to put humanity in the wrong. Many New Agers, particularly those with a Green consciousness, much prefer the idea of 'Goddess' to 'God'. They believe that Christianity has caused a great deal of psychological damage by the way in which it has refused to entertain the Goddess concept, and instead has presented the Blessed Virgin Mary as a female role model. So a wiccan New Ager can write that

> The ideal that Mary portrays is that of a desexualized woman and it denies the value of human relationship . . . For a man this image raised impossible problems in his relations with women . . . For a woman the Mary cult created an image of a 'perfect' woman to which she must aspire. The Virgin Mary is a woman without sin who achieves this perfection by submitting entirely to her husband and male God, serving them devotedly and seeking nothing for herself. A woman was not to gain wholeness through her own achievements and finding her own destiny. No divinity was made in her image. Her only role was to serve men.[14]

(Never mind, for the moment, what a travesty of Christian teaching this quotation represents. If that is how we appear to outsiders, we have got to take the fact of that image on board before we can do anything to alter it.)

Since God is all that is, there is nothing that is not God. There is no transcendent Other, and we ourselves are – like the rest of the cosmos – a part of the universal divinity. It is therefore not only allowable but proper to worship oneself, though the Self that one worships is not that fragment of individuality which distinguishes oneself from others, but the inherent god within all Selves.

New Age has room for community and celebration, but not for church and worship as understood by Christians. The typical New Ager wishes to be free, not only from the terrors of isolation, but also from the captivity to churches and institutions. That is why the New Age prefers to work through a network rather than within an organization. Insofar as there is any worship in New Age circles, it will be that of the individual who realizes and celebrates the mystical sense of unity with the Cosmos in a way like that expressed by Wordsworth:

> And I have felt
> A presence that disturbs me with the joy
> Of elevated thoughts; a sense sublime
> Of something far more deeply interfused,
> Whose dwelling is the light of setting suns.[15]

So worship is very definitely a thing which the individual will do in his solitariness; a matter of connecting 'the alone to the Alone' rather than of relating a community to the Trinity. There are moments of mystic unity with Self, God, and Nature, but since these cannot be forecast or manipulated, they have to be allowed to happen when they will. In the age of Aquarius, the spirit is poured out freely, so that set liturgy at set times, in conjunction with other people who have prearranged to be with one at the same place and the same time, is out of place (except in those branches of Wicca which are particularly keen on observing times and seasons).

New Agers will, in any case, not believe in corporate worship, preferring practice to mere profession, and being ready to accuse Christian worshippers of the Sunday hypocrisy which makes religion a thing of the tongue rather than of the truth. In any case, they do not believe that truth can reside in an institution – that is all of a piece with their distrust of dogma. Truth, if it is to be found at all, is to be found in the individual's apprehension of it. (Lack of enthusiasm for the Church, and preference for celebrating the destiny of the individual, is not a new phenomenon. Admirers of Beethoven's *Missa Solemnis* may recollect that he squeezes the words *unam sanctam catholicam et apostolicam ecclesiam* into three insignificant bars of the tenor line, but requires every voice in the chorus, all four soloists, and the whole orchestra to hammer away for sixteen pages of the Novello vocal score before he has said all he wants to say about *vitam venturi saeculi*.)

A further corollary of a doctrine of pantheism is that the Cosmos is seen as basically good, and there is no such 'thing' as evil. Evil is due to ignorance, and is banished by the acquisition of knowledge – knowledge, not of brute facts (which have little significance) but of one's true nature and its relationship to Reality.

> There is only God, only the 'Atma' or Essence. Everything that seems otherwise is the result of the way it is viewed, not its reality ... [Ultimate Good] is, simply, the truth, that which *is*. The opposite of that which is, is that which *is not*, i.e. non-existent ...

The devil does not lie outside us, hoofed and horned; he represents that in us which has not discovered the truth, and therefore does not act from truth, but from ignorance.[16]

New Agers are an eclectic mix of people, so we would not expect to find a logical consistency throughout New Age teaching. Despite the belief that there is nothing but God (the doctrine which philosophers call 'monism'), and that we partake of divinity by the very fact of existing, many New Agers will talk of a series of levels or planes between God and us, and of a hierarchy of Masters and Teachers. This is especially true of New Age circles influenced by Theosophy and the writings of Alice Bailey, though the idea of there being seven planes between the world of matter and the ultimate world is met elsewhere in New Age writings. The explanatory notes to one set of Tarot cards, for instance, point out that the Fool is represented as entering into manifestation with the radiance of his divinity still shining about him, 'but the memories are fading fast under the influence of his fall into matter'.[17] The idea of a 'fall' into matter is a far cry from saying that we all partake of divinity and that the earth and the matter in it is as divine as we are.

Finally, however, many New Agers would like to find a place in their scheme for Jesus of Nazareth. But it is not the place which Christians find for him. 'Christ' is the name of a person or entity with a particular cosmic role. Jesus is, for New Agers, at most the Christ of the Piscean Age (or even simply *one* of the Christs of the Piscean Age, or the Christ to whom we happen to relate). As the *Manual for Teachers* of *A Course in Miracles* says (my italics), 'Christ takes many forms with different names until their oneness can be recognized. But Jesus is *for you* the bearer of Christ's single message of the Love of God.'

Other New Agers see it as positively harmful to hang on to a reverence for the outmoded Jesus. Hugh de Cruz of the 'New Age Universal Christianity without Religion' praises Sananda, which is the Aquarian Age name of 'the former Jesus of the by gone Piscean Age of crucifixes and churchianity'. Still others have a respect for Jesus, but believe that, in the Aquarian Age, we may well need another Christ:

Many people within the New Age movement, primarily those with a theosophical background, see the necessity of the manifestation of a world teacher – a new avatar, an embodiment of God, a being of the status of Jesus or Gautama Buddha – who will be a catalyst to bring about the New Age ... The idea originated within the Esoteric Section of the Theosophical Society.[18]

This links up with ideas of the coming Maitreya and the claims made by Benjamin Creme about his imminent manifestation. There are affinities here with the belief in certain unorthodox Muslim circles (the Ahmadiyya) that the Koranic Sura 61.6 really teaches that there is a new Messiah, yet to come. The Ahmadiyya are to Islam rather as the Mormons are to Christianity, and one of their beliefs is that Jesus did not die on the cross, but travelled to Kashmir, where his tomb may be seen to this day.[19]

Other New Agers, as we have seen, try to rewrite the accounts of the life of Jesus as given in the Gospels in order to make them more palatable. The curious may consult Douglas Groothuis' *Revealing the New Age Jesus* for details.

A great deal of all the foregoing is redolent of gnostic views of the nature of God and his relation to the created world, except that the gnostics of earlier centuries would not have been as abashed as today's New Agers to be described as 'dogmatic'. Some New Agers, indeed, as Wesley Carr points out, specifically look towards the second-century gnostics as their inspiration.[20]

What did the gnostics teach? The gnostic movement of the early Christian centuries was as varied as the New Age movement of the twentieth, but all forms of it shared certain common basic convictions. As summarized by Professor James D. G. Dunn, they are as follows:

(1) A sharp dualism between spirit and matter, and between the upper world and the lower world. Spirit alone was of heaven and good. Matter was of the lower world, corrupted and evil. (2) The soul was a divine spark in man, a piece of heavenly spirit fallen to earth and imprisoned within the material body, enclosed and stifled by the despised 'mud' of the flesh. (3) Salvation consisted in recalling the soul to its true nature by providing it with knowledge (Greek, *'gnosis'*) of its true home and with instructions on the way back to the upper world. In Christian gnosticism the Christian element added to the syncretistic mix was (4) belief in Christ as a heavenly being who came down to earth to give the vital *gnosis* to the lost souls.'[21]

Very many of these gnostic ideas are taken up in only slightly different forms in a great deal of New Age teaching.[22]

Where did gnosticism come from? From time to time in New Age literature, we come across claims that gnostic ideas represent the original Christianity but that someone (it may have been Paul or it may have been an anonymous mafia within the Church of the late first or second centuries) decided to change things; the original documents were doctored and their ideas repressed so successfully that nothing of the 'real', original faith remained for later centuries to read, until an ancient gnostic library turned up in the soil of Nag Hammadi in Egypt in 1945.

That scenario cannot be sustained on the basis of sound scholarship. Admittedly the Nag Hammadi documents have taught us more about the real beliefs of at least some gnostics than we previously suspected – after all, until we had them, we had to rely almost entirely on descriptions of gnosticism written by Christian controversialists whose business it was to make gnostic ideas sound as ridiculous as possible. But that still leaves open the question of gnostic origins. The most that can reasonably be claimed is that here are ideas which were being canvassed by speculative groups of early Christians in an attempt to interpret the New Testament in ways more congenial to the thought-world of the Mediterranean culture of their time. Gnosticism is a post-New-Testament Christian heresy, and has no connection with New Testament origins. That is the view of Simone Petrement. Most historians of doctrine disagree and see gnosticism as having even less connection with the New Testament than that. Far from its arising as a specifically Christian heresy, they hold that gnosticism 'has far deeper roots in non-Christian Judaism than in Christianity, and that many Christian elements in gnostic texts are often only secondary trimmings'.[23]

Either way, any attempt to claim gnostic teachings as original Christianity is doomed to failure. The truth of it is that some New Age ideas are similar to some gnostic ones which tried unsuccessfully to hijack Christianity in its early years. They have no connection with what Jesus of Nazareth taught. As to their own truth or error, they have to be judged on their own merits as yet one more alternative to Christianity.

If all these ideas which we have been examining are basic manifestations of New Age thinking, what are they saying to the Christian Church? *Manifold Wisdom: Christians and the New Age* by Wesley Carr, the Dean of Bristol, has a good many insights for Christians approaching this task. My own list of *desiderata* would include the following:

The first thing to acknowledge is that many of the concerns of the New Age are legitimate, and that the Christian Church does not have a very good past record on them. It is right to have a concern for the future of that part of the created order which shares Planet Earth with us, and Christian teaching in past generations on the relation of humanity to the rest of creation contains much of which we need to repent. It is right that we should teach human beings to walk tall, as people who deserve affirmation and respect, and wrong to use religious beliefs in a way which makes them feel unworthy and second-class. It is right to insist that all human beings – whatever their class or colour or gender – are equally valuable in God's sight, and wrong that the Church should be seen as the place where respectable middle-class Westerners are ministered to by a male élite. It is right to look for a way through the barren and loveless materialism of so much of late twentieth-century Western culture, and it is a disaster that those who seek spirituality should come to feel that they will not find what they are looking for in the Church. It is right that people should seek for a faith to live by, that they should ask questions and not automatically take the answers that past tradition or present authority insists upon; and sad that they find the Church a place where dogmatic affirmations have to be accepted without questioning, and seekers are discouraged unless they tread well-worn and well-signposted tracks.

Why have New Agers either left the Church or not even considered it as an option on their spiritual odyssey? Lowell Streiker suggests four possible reasons:

1. They grew up within the Church and found it irrelevant.
2. They have only met Christianity as a 'civil religion' without heart or soul.
3. They had 'intimations of eternity' but the Church was not interested in them.
4. They have had transforming experiences, and see the Church as an enemy and a target.

He goes on:

For the most part New Agers cannot find the holy in the church or in any of its versions of what is real and important. Yet, followers of the New Age are burned and singed by the presence of the holy in their lives ... There are moments of bliss and beatitude as well as depths of despair and aloneness . . . Grains of living truth explode and burn with incandescence through the air, . . . [but] the sands that the church filters are, for the devotees of the New Age, dead ash, glowing with not even the embers of the Real.[24]

There is much about the Church which New Agers find profoundly unattractive. They have drunk from the numinous springs of religious experience, they want to understand what has happened to them and to integrate it within a total view which gives meaning to their life, and what do they see? A declining organization trying to raise money to keep ugly Victorian buildings open for a knot of dull people to come and spend an hour there on a wet Sunday morning. A group of people engaged in hurling sectarian abuse at other groups of people, who seem to the outsider to be indistinguishable from the first group. A body which is tearing itself apart by doctrinal disputes about who is or is not genetically qualified to pronounce certain words in a church service. The Church is being judged, and it is not coming out of the experience in a good light. We who stay within the Church may say that all this criticism is unfair, and that if people only joined us, they would find things otherwise. Is this true? Ought we not to acknowledge that sometimes we are being rightly condemned and that those who look on us from outside and want nothing to do with us have some justification for their attitudes?

The most serious accusation – and there is some truth in it – is that the Church is embarrassed by religious experience. It has domesticated the holy, and only made it acceptable if it is expressed in certain stylized ways. We need to work towards a Church where it can be taken for granted that there are people who have disturbing glimpses of something strangely numinous which lies behind the translucent veils of everyday life; but that we should not necessarily expect such moments to be expressed in terms which can be entombed within a prepackaged doctrinal system. God may touch human beings with his Spirit, and surprise them with joy. We ought to expect such moments to come, and be ready to share them without embarrassment within the whole Christian community, where we can then explore them in openness and humility. The same goes for psychic experiences, which can be disturbing for those who do not know how to integrate them within a total (and totally Christian) theology.

But we shall – quite definitely and rightly – explore them within a dogmatic Church. That word 'dogma' has sadly altered its meaning over the centuries. The Shorter Oxford English Dictionary gives its original meaning as 'that which is held as an opinion'. Certainly that is the derivation of the word, from the Greek *dokein*, 'to think, suppose, imagine, expect', and *dogma*, 'that which seems to me, an opinion'. There is a famous use of the word *dokein* in Acts 15.28, where the decision of the Council was expressed in the words 'It *seemed good* to the Holy Ghost, and to us' (AV – the REB translates it as, 'It is the decision of the Holy Spirit, and our decision'). The trouble began when Christians turned opinions into doctrines, and required all baptized members of the Church formally to declare their adherence to them.

It is not an easy matter to resolve. As the Editor of the *Expository Times* recently wrote: 'Every attempt at defining doctrine is bound to divide Christians and to mislead human beings into thinking that they can set out the whole nature of God in a few written statements. On the other hand truth and identity do matter.' He goes on to speculate that 'perhaps even the question of whether Christianity has been right to place orthodox belief in the centre needs to be debated more seriously.'[25]

His remark arose from a statement by Professor Frances Young, who wrote that 'Christianity is the only major religion to set such store by creeds and doctrines'. Other religions have scriptures, ways of worship, ethics and lifestyles, hymns and prayers, festivals and popular myths; but, she points out, 'except in response to Christianity, they have not developed creeds, statements of standard belief to which the orthodox are supposed to adhere ... They have no "orthodoxy", a sense of right belief which is doctrinally sound and from which deviation means heresy.'[26]

The way in which the Nicene Creed is used in the Rite A Holy Communion service of the Church of England's *Alternative Service Book 1980* seems to get it just about right. It begins '*We* believe'. The 'we' does not primarily refer to the individual members of the particular congregation which is using those words at that particular moment. It refers to the whole Christian Church, throughout the world and throughout its history. It is only fair that the Church should declare, as dogma, what has 'seemed to it' over the centuries to be the basic irreducible minimum of what constitutes Christianity. That way, no one needs to be left in doubt as to what is the public teaching of the Church and what is the private opinion of its members – even of its current leaders. Christianity is the faith of the

Church. You cannot add to it or subtract from it and still call what is left 'Christianity'.

There are plenty of people (and many of them have belonged to Christian congregations for years) who cannot personally affirm the whole of the Creed as a matter of their own inner conviction. They should not therefore be debarred from joining in Christian worship, nor from repeating the Creed. What, in effect, they say when they do so, is that they recognize that the Church has (and should have) a stance on matters of doctrine. The Church's stance will not in every detail reflect the personal opinion of every member of the assembly or satisfy every worshipper as an explanation of his experiences. But the congregation believes it can explore into God by being a body which uses these words to express its corporate and historical convictions.

If this is how we regard the use of the Creed in Christian worship, we are taking the sting out of 'dogma' and recognizing that the church is a place where spiritual seekers are welcome. The Church is a place where we should be able to find spiritual liberty. Jesus Christ frees; he does not enslave. We find it easy to be enslaved either within our own ideas or within a dogmatic system which allows no room for dissidents. If we work towards the goal of having a Church which is a glorious example of this freedom which Christ brings, it will not only be more attractive to outsiders who might otherwise leave it for New Age groups; it will also be healthier in itself, and (one prays) truer to its Founder and to the God to whom it bears witness. The whole of *Free to Believe*, by David and Rebecca Jenkins, is a passionate and deeply Christian argument in favour of dogma without dogmatism.

What aspects of Christian belief, then, do we need to emphasize in the light of distortions which have caused New Agers to prefer their own version of the nature of reality?

The Church believes in a transcendent Creator God who may be found through his creation but who is separate from it. We cannot, therefore, properly worship the creation or any part of it, and we cannot identify God by any description of the creation, however exhaustive. In other words, God is *in* his creation (panentheism) but the creation is not God (which would be pantheism). Within this creation there may be many wonderful things – God is creator 'of all that is, seen and unseen'. If we wish to believe in the existence of nature spirits such as the *devas* of Findhorn, there is nothing in the Christian faith to prevent us from doing so; but if we do, we will recognize them as part of God's creation, and anything we learn from them we will check out before we believe it, because we know that there are parts of the creation which no longer obey the laws of their creator, and we need therefore to exercise discrimination.

The Church believes that human beings (men and women together) have been made in the image of this Creator God. The great Christian mystics, particularly Meister Eckhart in the fourteenth century, had a doctrine of *synteresis*, which expressed the idea that a divine spark exists in every human being; but that is not the same as saying that every human being is a part of God. We can find God within our fellows, as we can find God in and through nature; but we cannot say that they (or we) are a part of that divinity. It means, however, that we are justified in using human analogies to describe the nature of this God, even if they are only analogies and not descriptions, so that we have to look at them carefully and see where they break down.

One such analogy is personhood or personality, so that we can rightly describe God in personal terms and it would be wrong to describe him as an impersonal Force or Power. But the analogy cannot be taken too far, and eventually breaks down, because personality is too limiting a concept to apply to God. This is expressed by saying that he is *at least* personal, but that human ideas of personality do not exhaust our description of him.

Another such analogy is fatherhood. This must not be held to imply that we believe in a male God; only that the concept of fatherhood has been found to be particularly useful in describing some of the ways in which we come to know God and his relationship with us. In particular, it does not mean that there is any need to complete the description of God by positing another being of goddess stature, or by saying that the earth or any other part of the creation is a goddess. It *does* mean that, because the Father analogy is imperfect and incomplete, we need to recognize the feminine attributes to God – the *same* God – and to find other analogies which we have to use when speaking of him/her. Since they, too, are analogies, we will need to beware of taking them too literally. At least they will help to prevent us from making the analogy of fatherhood too masculine and overbearing.

If God is Creator, then we believe we can look at creation and find out things about him. We will respect the created order, the planet and everything on it, both living and inanimate. It is a Christian thing to pursue Green policies and to do as little harm to the earth as we can. We will treat it with consideration, though we will not need to be any more sentimental about it than the creation is sentimental in itself. Creation is prodigal, and species come and go. None is sacrosanct, and in a world of limited size, evolution can only proceed by the elimination of species which are steps on the way of development. God can love, and have a purpose for, things which pass away. He is above both time and eternity, and therefore the things which he created do not have to partake of God's eternity before they can have a value to him.

God has created humankind. That means that we have a place in the purpose of God, and we can walk tall in his sight. Every human being is of infinite worth in the eyes of God – a truth expressed in traditional theology by saying that God thinks each human being is worth dying for. Any theology which tries to belittle humanity, or any religious practice which succeeds in making people feel unworthy, is therefore in itself an unworthy theology. The God who became incarnate in Jesus can become the God within everyone of us – 'Christ in you, the hope of a glory to come' (Col. 1.27). 'We know that when Christ appears we shall be like him, because we shall see him as he is' (1 Jn 3.2). Meanwhile, supremely in the sacrament of the Eucharist, we take his life within ours as the first instalment of a glorification which will be consummated at the end of all the ages, when 'God will be all, and in all' (1 Cor. 15.28). Christians who are tempted towards a religion which brings them low self-esteem would do well to meditate on these texts, and then read Francis Dewar's *Live for a Change*, especially the chapter headed 'Know Your Gifts'.

This world, and the people within it, however, are not perfect. There are many ways of explaining the presence of evil, but no Christian theology can deny it, or say that it is unreal, or hold that it is a manifestation simply of ignorance. The devils who oppose God do not do so out of ignorance – they believe in God, and it makes them tremble, as James 2.19 puts it. Yes, eventually evil *will* disappear, but only when everything in Creation has come to a complete knowledge of God and his ways, and that will take place (at the end of history) not through education but through a moral process.

Meanwhile, evil is engrained within humanity and has tainted the whole world. This has to be recognized as a fact, and religion must provide some way of coming to terms with it. The Christian religion does it by showing how the rebellion of humanity against its Creator had to be answered, not by an effort of the created order (which was too far gone to save itself), but through God's own initiative in coming in person to the earth he had made. We cannot satisfactorily explain the state of the world and the relation of God to it without a doctrine of incarnation.

That incarnation of God into his world came about in Jesus of Nazareth, the Christ of God. He is to be seen in cosmic terms. Whoever wrote the letter to Colossae saw him as 'the image of the invisible God' and went on (1. 15–17) to say that

> his is the primacy over all creation. In him, everything in heaven and on earth was created, not only things visible but also the invisible orders of thrones, sovereignties, authorities, and powers: the whole universe has been created through him and for him. He exists before all things, and all things are held together in him.

At the time when the Christian faith was beginning to make its way in the world, the idea that world history could be divided into ages was a common one. The earliest Christians believed that a new age had begun with the coming of Jesus, so that they were in the period when the old and the new ages were overlapping (one translation of 1 Cor. 10.11 speaks of Christians as those who are living 'in the overlap of the ages'). They did not think of this New Age as a temporary one; it was the final age. Nor did they expect any further Word to come from God to supersede the Word incarnate in Jesus. He was the Lord of the new age which began when God came down to earth. Christians believe that Jesus is the Lord of our present age because we are still in the age of the incarnation. He will be the Lord of any age, because he is the Lord of all ages, until the Final Day, when God will be all, and in all. God's purposes for eternity have been revealed in time, and what has been accomplished through Jesus will last until time itself comes to an end.

Incarnation means that this cosmic figure became a real human being – flesh, no less (John 1.14). The Letter to Hebrews shows how we need to hold both aspects of this great paradox in a profound synthesis if we are properly to see who this person was, who, though 'he is the radiance of God's glory, the stamp of God's very being, and he sustains the universe by his word of power' (Heb. 1.3), yet had to 'learn obedience through his suffering' (Heb. 5.8).[27]

The Church, finally, teaches that when God did become incarnate, he was not taken seriously, but was put to death on the cross. The doctrine of atonement, which is central and essential to Christianity, shows that forgiveness is not an immoral way in which God decides to turn a blind eye to the misdemeanours of humanity. It shows that forgiveness is a costly business. Anyone who complains that the forgiveness of sins is immoral because we can be forgiven simply by 'saying we are sorry' has not begun to consider either the gravity of sin which required a death on the cross to disempower it, or the seriousness of repentance, which needs to be accompanied by a realization of how great the love of God must be if he is in fact able to offer us forgiveness in the way that he does.

If these doctrines were emphasized, and if more Christians lived as though they believed they were true, it would show that the Christian faith is the answer to the spiritual search of the New Age movement, as of every religious quest. In the last few pages, I have done little more than state, briefly and baldly, what Christianity teaches. The end of a book in which I have tried to understand the New Age is not the place for a detailed essay in systematic theology. Suffice it to say that in my opinion, Christianity is a coherent system of belief which can answer to the deepest needs of the whole of humanity, and it deserves to outlast the New Age movement.

Not only does it deserve to do so, it will; both because it is a 'more excellent way', and also because 'The Way' is one of the titles of Jesus, who is the cosmic Christ of this and every age, to whom be the glory – to the ages of the ages!

Notes

(For details of works cited, see the Bibliography following. Except where otherwise stated, all biblical quotations are taken from the Revised English Bible, © Oxford University Press and Cambridge University Press, 1989.)

Chapter 1
1 Jacob Needleman, quoted in Klimo, p. 9.
2 'At even, ere the sun was set', by H. Twells (1868).
3 Seddon, p. 3.
4 See Carr, p. xii.

Chapter 2
1 Irwin, p. 7.
2 C. G. Jung, *Flying Saucers: A Modern Myth*, para. 589 (p. 311). I am grateful to my friend Geoffrey West for tracking down this quotation for me.
3 Ferguson, p. 27.
4 The title of a book by Maurice Cooke (Marcus Books 1983), quoted by Klimo, p. 61, n9.
5 Ferguson, p. 148.
6 ibid., p. 155.
7 ibid., p. 156.
8 ibid., p. 83.
9 William McCready, quoted Ferguson, p. 401.
10 For much of what follows, see Drury; I am grateful to Paul Heelas for putting me on to this account of the human potential movement.
11 A. J. Sutich, in a dissertation presented to the Humanistic Psychology Institute, as quoted by Drury, p. 38.
12 Drury, p. 103.
13 ibid., p. 124.
14 ibid., p. 104.
15 Irwin, p. 101.
16 Starhawk, reprinted in Bloom, pp. 34–5.
17 Levine, reprinted in Bloom, pp. 105–6.
18 Streiker, p. 163.
19 Newbigin, p. 139. He was writing about pluralism in general, but the quotation is particularly apposite in this specific context.

Chapter 3
1 Streiker, p. 160.
2 Bloom (1), pp. xv–xvi.
3 Scott, p. 5. My thanks to Arnold Taylor for furnishing me with this quotation.
4 Huxley, p. 1.
5 Klimo, p. 297.
6 Melton (1), p. 127.
7 Bloom (1), pp. xvii–xviii.
8 Brochure of the Natale Institute (UK), 73 York Way, London N7 9QF.
9 Bloom (1), p. 153.
10 Montgomery, pp. 30–1, quoted by Klimo, p. 126.
11 As quoted in *Light*, vol. 111, No. 1 (Spring 1991), pp. 36–7.
12 For examples, see Seddon, p. 13.
13 *Leading Edge* (for address, see Bibliography below).
14 For details, consult *Alternatives*, St James's Church, 197 Piccadilly, London W1V 9LF.
15 Scientific and Medical Network, 9 Julier House, Pera Road, Bath BA1 5PA.
16 Financial difficulties have forced the Wrekin Trust into virtual hibernation for an estimated 18 months from late 1991 onwards, though many of its conferences and courses have been transferred to other organizations. Correspondence is still being dealt with at Runnings Park, Croft Bank, West Malvern, Worcs., WR14 4BP.
17 Irwin, p. 80.

Chapter 4
1 Melton (2), p. 277.
2 Liz Greene, 'The Planetary Map of Human Potential', in Bloom (1), p. 45.
3 ibid., p. 43.
4 Jones, pp. 2–3.
5 Fenton, p. 143.
6 ibid., p. 8.
7 See Ridder-Patrick for details.
8 Melton (2), p. 277.
9 Cassidy, p. 17.
10 Green, p. 167.
11 Peach, p. 17.
12 ibid.; her italics.
13 e.g., Drury, pp. 73–8; Peach, *passim*.
14 Mathers, p. x.
15 Melton (2), p. 135.
16 *I Ching or Book of Changes* (Arkana, 1989).
17 Green, p. 147.
18 Klimo, p. 198.
19 Perry (1), pp. 49–50.

20 Green, p. 102.
21 See McClure for the whole story.
22 See Tart for a discriminating analysis.
23 Moss gives much of the early story.
24 Professor Cedric Wilson's work is especially interesting. See Wilson and Perry.

Chapter 5
1 Adams; see also Irwin, p. 26. Dr Adams apparently now believes that Power Socket Radiation can be blocked by aluminium foil – see the *Scientific and Medical Network Newsletter* (9 Julier House, Pera Road, Bath BA1 5PA), No. 46 (August 1991), pp. 28–9.
2 Carr, p. 124.
3 Roney-Dougal, pp. 233f (n16).
4 Irwin, p. 27.
5 ibid., pp. 10–11.
6 ibid., p. 36.
7 ibid., p. 22.

Chapter 6
1 For examples, see Thomas.
2 A transcript of the trial is given in Roberts.
3 Halsbury's *Statutes of England and Wales* (Butterworth), 4th edn, vol.12, p. 234n.
4 Green, p. 11.
5 Luhrmann, p. 109.
6 Roney-Dougal, p. 37.
7 A good introduction is to be found in Crowley.
8 For a general view, see Green.
9 ibid., p. 11.
10 Roney-Dougal, pp. 179–82.
11 Green, p. 7.
12 Anderson, p. 13.
13 Roney-Dougal, p. 208.
14 Crowley, pp. 163–4.
15 Livesey, pp. 73–5.
16 Green, p. 18.
17 ibid., p. 17.
18 Roney-Dougal, p. 158.
19 Spink (1), pp. 100–1.
20 ibid., p. 101.
21 Roney-Dougal, pp. 140, 158.
22 ibid., p. 162.
23 Green, p. 89.
24 Luhrmann, p. 110.
25 Green, pp. 99f.
26 Luhrmann, p. 111.

27 C. S. Rodd, *The Expository Times*, vol. 102, No. 9 (June 1991), p. 258.
28 See the Editorial in *The Christian Parapsychologist*, vol. 9, No. 3 (September 1991), pp. 74–5.
29 ORCRO magazine is available from BCM Gevurah, London WC1N 3XX.
30 *Fortean Times*, (20 Paul Street, Frome, Somerset BA11 1DX), No. 57 (Spring 1991), pp. 43–62.

Chapter 7
 1 Bradley, p. 13.
 2 Roney-Dougal, pp. 163–4.
 3 ibid., p. 166.
 4 See also, for a useful summary, Melton (2), pp. 401–4.
 5 Spink (2), p. 55.
 6 From Lovelock, 'Gaia', in Bloom, p. 166. See also Sheldrake.
 7 Lovelock, ibid., p. 167.
 8 From Sahtouris, 'Gaia's Dance', in Bloom, p. 168.
 9 From Rainbow Publications, PO Box 486, London SW1P 1AZ.
10 Spink (1), p. 98.
11 Roney-Dougal, p. 184.
12 Fox (2), p. 267.
13 ibid., p. 247.
14 ibid.
15 For a critique, see Brearley (my thanks to Paul Heelas for drawing this to my attention).
16 Seddon, p. 16.
17 Thomas Traherne, *Centuries of Meditations*, 3.2.
18 ibid., 3.3.
19 ibid., 1.14.
20 Pss. 19.1; 104.2, 21; 148.8; 65.13b–14 (PBV).
21 Joseph Addison in *The Spectator*, 23 August 1712, paraphrasing the opening verses of Ps. 19.
22 Charleston, p. 7.
23 ibid., p. 8.
24 The full text is on sale at many Earthcare or New Age shops; it is also given in *Areopagus*, vol. 4, No. 2 (Lent 1991), pp. 10–11.
25 Seddon, p. 17.

Chapter 8
 1 Book V, Chapter 12 (*Penguin Classics* edn, pp. 289–94).
 2 PO Box 7767, Philadelphia, PA 19101–7767, USA; 9 Julier House, Pera Road, Bath BA1 5PA.
 3 Atwater gives a helpful discussion of the after-effects of the near-death experience.
 4 Ring and Rosing, p. 232.
 5 *Journal of Near-Death Studies*, vol. 7, No. 4 (Summer 1989), pp. 223–63.
 6 Weldon and Levitt, pp. 79, 85–7.

7 Ring (2), p. 239.
8 Ring (1), Chapter 8, 'Planetary Visions of Near–Death Experiencers'.
9 Lorimer, p. 257.
10 ibid., p. 90.
11 ibid., p. 91.
12 Ring (2), pp. 240–1.
13 A phrase used by Richard Bewes in the *Church of England Newspaper* for 1 December 1989, and quoted by Mitton and Parker, p. 19.
14 Mitton and Parker, pp. 18–19.
15 Nichelson, p. 204.

Chapter 9
1 As quoted in the Gallup Poll in the *Daily Telegraph* for 15 April 1979.
2 Lorimer, p. 107.
3 *Bhagavad Gita*, II, 22, quoted by Lorimer, p. 115.
4 S. Radhakrishnan, *History of Philosophy*, vol. 1, p. 165, quoted by Lorimer, p. 119.
5 For an exposition, see Butler, and also Christie-Murray.
6 The case is summarized in Ian Wilson, pp. 19–28, where a great deal of cold water is poured upon it.
7 Stevenson, *Children Who Remember Past Lives*, p. 158.
8 Perry (6), p. 168.
9 Tarazi, p. 309.
10 Perry (4), p. 177.
11 Reported in Ian Wilson, pp. 127–34.
12 Paramahansa Yogananda, quoted in Lorimer, p. 106.
13 Lorimer, p. 133.
14 See Perry (7).
15 Groothuis, p. 250.
16 William Wordsworth (1770–1850), *Intimations of Immortality*, v.
17 Perry (4), p. 183.

Chapter 10
1 Mascall and Jones, p. 31.
2 As claimed in *Light*, vol. 111, No. 1 (Spring 1991), p. 16.
3 The beginnings of Spiritualism are often dated to the Fox sisters' experiences in 1848, but for an earlier date for the start of the movement, see Nancy Zingrone in the *Journal of Parapsychology*, vol. 54, No. 4 (December 1990), p. 391, and Richard Winkelman in the *Journal of the American Society for Psychical Research*, vol. 85, No. 3 (July 1991), p. 312.
4 Maynard, pp. 31–46, quoted by Klimo, p. 100–1.
5 Bassett, p. 89. I am grateful to Leslie Price for this information.
6 *The Story of the White Eagle Lodge*, pp. 52–3.
7 SFFI, 3310 Baring Street, Philadelphia, PA 19104, or PO Box 7868, Philadelphia, PA 19101, USA; ARPR, PO Box 614, Bloomfield, CT 06002, USA.

8 See Stringfellow and Towne, or from a different standpoint, Pike.

9 CFPSS publishes a 'house journal', the *Quarterly Review*, and a theological quarterly, the *Christian Parapsychologist*. Both are free to members and associate members, and CP is also separately available on subscription from CFPSS, The Rural Workshop, South Road, North Somercotes, Louth, Lincolnshire LN11 7PT.

10 Moore, pp. 1–2.

11 The Report with commentary is available from the CFPSS (see note 9 above). See also editorials in *The Christian Parapyschologist*, vol. 8, No. 6 (June 1990), pp. 202–4, and vol. 9, No. 2 (June 1991), pp. 38–9. The quotation comes from paragraph 11(C) of the 1939 Report (p. 64, CFPSS edn).

12 *Survival of Death*, *Hidden Man*, and *Living On* (from the College of Psychic Studies, 16 Queensberry Place, London SW7 2EB).

13 See Cockerell for a theological assessment of Doris Stokes.

14 Klimo gives an excellent introduction to the whole subject. See also Hastings.

15 Northage, p. 28.

16 See Klimo, pp. 28–34.

17 Quoted ibid., p. 30.

18 Quoted ibid., p. 16.

19 Quoted ibid., p. 49.

20 ibid., pp. 48–9.

21 ibid., p. 183.

22 ibid., pp. 53–6.

23 See Wise for details.

24 There is an account in Cocks.

25 *A Course in Miracles*, vol. 1 (Text), pp. 6–7, 81, 113; Skutch, p. 60 (quoted by Klimo, p. 40).

26 ibid., (Text, pp. 52f., 358); quoted by Klimo, p. 39.

27 Brown, p. 4.

28 Carey, pp. 68–70, quoted by Klimo, pp. 58–9.

29 *Manual for Teachers of A Course in Miracles*, quoted Klimo, p. 41.

30 Mark 13. 21–2, REB translation, with the word 'Christ' substituted for 'Messiah'.

31 See Mircea Eliade's classic study, *Shamanism*.

32 Green, p. 159.

33 Fisher, p. 70.

34 Roney-Dougal, p. 40. See McIntosh for a comparison between the use of drugs in primitive cultures and that in the West of the 1960s.

35 See Abrahamson.

36 Lindblom, pp. 1–2.

37 Numbers 22.2 – 24.25.

38 2 Kings 22.

39 1 Corinthians 12.28–29; 14.1.

40 Lindblom, pp. 18–26.

41 Perry (3).

42 Tyrrell, p. 30.
43 Klimo, p. 296.
44 ibid., p. 256.
45 Hastings, *Noetic Sciences Review* (Spring/Summer 1991), p. 11.
46 See, for example, David Lewis's chapter, '"Spiritual Powers" – Real or Counterfeit?' in Cole *et al.*, pp. 109–25.
47 Alice A. Bailey, *Telepathy* (Lucis 1950), pp. 75–7, quoted by Klimo, p. 321.
48 Klimo, p. 321.
49 Spink (1), p. 76.

Chapter 11
  1 Denton, (Briefing Paper No. 2 [May 1990]), pp. 11–12.
  2 Livesey, p. 121.
  3 ibid., p. 123.
  4 Denton, (Briefing Paper No. 2 [May 1990]), pp. 12–13.
  5 Livesey, p. 4.
  6 Schlink, p. 7.
  7 ibid., p. 8.
  8 ibid., p. 11.
  9 Cole *et al.*, Chapter 7.
10 Vol. 6, No. 5 (August/September 1990), published by PWM, 175 Tower Bridge Road, London SE1 2AB.
11 Spink (2), p. 85.
12 ibid., pp. i, 8.
13 ibid. p. 9.
14 Spink (1), p. 8.
15 ibid., p. 15.
16 ibid., p. 97.
17 Spink (2), pp. 13f.
18 Spink (3), p. 52.
19 An exposition of the Enneagram is to be found in Palmer.
20 Innes, p. 31.
21 *Christianity and the New Age* (Minton House, Findhorn, Forres, Moray, Scotland, 1990).

Chapter 12
  1 Riddell, p. 87.
  2 Spink (1), p. 4.
  3 'It came upon the midnight clear.' The hymn was written in the mid-nineteenth century by E. H. Sears, an American Unitarian.
  4 Thorne, p. 20.
  5 Roney-Dougal, p. 179.
  6 Nineham, p. 313.
  7 Cited by W. W. Bartley, *Werner Erhard* (1978), pp. 166–8; quoted by Heelas. My italics.
  8 Melton (2), p. 304.

9 For this whole paragraph, see Heelas.
10 Riddell, p. 132.
11 ibid., p. 30.
12 See Chapter 3 above, pp. 32–3.
13 Riddell, p. 30.
14 Crowley, pp. 163–4.
15 William Wordsworth, *Lines composed ... above Tintern Abbey*, lines 93–7.
16 Riddell, pp. 30–1.
17 Ashcroft-Nowicki (1).
18 Melton (2), p. 305.
19 See Opsal for details.
20 Carr, pp. 104–5.
21 Dunn, pp. 96–7.
22 Groothuis, Chapter 4 (pp. 73–100).
23 See Tuckett.
24 Streiker, pp. 151–2.
25 Editorial in the *Expository Times*, vol. 102, No. 9 (June 1991), p. 258.
26 Young, Chapter 1.
27 See Perry (2).

Bibliography

A *list of books, pamphlets, articles, and periodicals quoted or mentioned in the text.*

Robert-Louis Abrahamson, 'The Silence of Mature Prayer', *Theology*, vol. 94, No. 757 (January–February 1991), pp. 39–46.

Mike Adams, 'Crystal Antidotes to Power Socket Radiation', *Leading Edge*, No. 3 (Spring 1991), pp. 7, 23.

William Anderson, *Green Man: The Archetype of our Oneness with the Earth*. HarperCollins 1990.

Areopagus: A Living Encounter with Today's Religious World, published quarterly by the Tao Fong Shan Christian Centre, PO Box 33, Shatin, NT, Hong Kong.

Dolores Ashcroft-Nowicki (1), *The Servants of the Light Tarot*. Aquarian Press 1991.

Dolores Ashcroft-Nowicki (2), *The Tree of Ecstasy*. Aquarian Press 1991.

P. M. H. Atwater, *Coming Back to Life: The Aftereffects of the Near Death Experience*. Ballentyne, New York, 1989.

Randall N. Baer, *Inside the New Age Nightmare*. Huntington House, Inc., distributed in UK by Diasozo Trust, Erith, Kent, 1989.

Richard N. Bailey, Eric Cambridge, and H. Denis Briggs, *Dowsing and Church Archaeology*. Intercept 1988.

Jean Bassett, *One Hundred Years of National Spiritualism*. Headquarters Publishing Co. 1990.

Susan Blackmore, 'A Psychological Theory of the Out-of-Body Experience', *Journal of Parapsychology*, vol. 48, No. 3 (September 1984), pp. 201–18.

G. B. Blaker, 'Kirlian Photography', *Quarterly Review* of the Churches' Fellowship for Psychical and Spiritual Studies, No. 89 (Autumn 1976), pp. 7–11.

William Bloom (1), ed., *The New Age: An Anthology of Essential Writings*. Rider 1991.

William Bloom (2), *Sacred Times: A New Approach to Festivals*. Findhorn Press 1990.

Ian Bradley, *God is Green*. Darton Longman & Todd 1990.

Margaret Brearley, 'Matthew Fox: Creation Spirituality for the Aquarian Age', *Christian/Jewish Relations*, vol. 22, No. 2 (1989), pp. 37–49.

H. Denis Briggs, 'Dowsing techniques applied to church archaeology', *The Christian Parapsychologist*, vol. 8, No. 7 (September 1990), pp. 234–42.

Rebecca Brown, *He Came to Set the Captives Free*. Chick Publications, Chino, California, 1986.

Edwin Butler, 'Serial Consciousness', *Light*, vol. 98, No. 1 (Spring 1978), pp. 17–24.

Ken Carey, *The Starseed Transmissions*. Kansas City 1982.

Wesley Carr, *Manifold Wisdom: Christians in the New Age* SPCK 1991.

Philip Carr-Gomm, *The Elements of the Druid Tradition*. Element Books 1991.

L. L. Cassidy, 'The believing Christian as a dedicated astrologer', *The Astrological Review* (1978), reprinted in *The Christian Parapyschologist*, vol. 7, No. 1 (March 1987), pp. 12–18.

Steven Charleston, 'American Indian Tradition – Rediscovering an Old Testament', *Areopagus*, vol. 4, No. 1 (Lent 1991), pp. 5–8.

The Christian Parapsychologist. Address as at note 9 to Chapter 10, above.

David Christie-Murray, 'The Evidence for Reincarnation', *Psychical Studies*, No. 32 (Summer 1983), pp. 1–14.

David Cockerell, 'The Art of Doris Stokes', *Theology*, vol. 90, No. 734 (March 1987), pp. 120–6.

Michael Cocks, 'St Stephen speaks', *The Christian Parapsychologist*, vol. 4, No. 2 (June 1981), pp. 38–44.

Michael Cole, Jim Graham, Tony Higton, and David Lewis, *What is the New Age?*. Hodder & Stoughton 1990.

A Course in Miracles. Arkana 1984.

Vivianne Crowley, *Wicca: The Old Religion in a New Age*. Aquarian Press 1989.

Constance Cumbey, *The Hidden Dangers of the Rainbow: The New Age Movement and our Coming Age of Barbarism*. Shreveport, Louisiana, Huntington House, 1983.

Clifford Denton, *A Christian Response to the New Age Movement*. PWM Trust, 175 Tower Bridge Road, London SE1 2AB, 1990.

Francis Dewar, *Live for a Change*. Darton, Longman & Todd 1988.

Nevill Drury, *The Elements of Human Potential*. Element Books 1989.

James D. G. Dunn, *The Evidence for Jesus*. SCM Press 1985.

Evangelical Alliance (186 Kennington Park Road, London SE1 4BT), *New Age Promise – Age Old Problem?* (1990).

The Evangelical Outlook, 2300 Ninth Street South, Suite 301, Arlington, VA 22204–2351, USA.

The Expository Times, T. & T. Clark, 59 George Street, Edinburgh EH2 2LQ.

H. J. Eysenck and D. K. B. Nias, *Astrology – Science or Superstition?* Penguin Books 1983.

Sasha Fenton, *Understanding Astrology*. Aquarian Press 1991.
Marilyn Ferguson, *The Aquarian Conspiracy*. Routledge & Kegan Paul 1981.
Joe Fisher, *Hungry Ghosts*. Grafton (Collins) 1990.
Matthew Fox (1), *Creation Spirituality: Liberating Gifts for the People of the Earth*. HarperSanFrancisco 1991.
Matthew Fox (2), *Original Blessing*. Santa Fe, New Mexico, Bear & Co., 1983; UK edn, Element Books 1989.

Michel Gauquelin, *The Scientific Basis for Astrology*. 1969.
Marian Green, *A Witch Alone*. Aquarian Press 1991.
Liz Greene, *Relating – An Astrological Guide to Living with Others*. Aquarian Press 1986.
Margot Grey, *Return from Death*. Arkana 1985.
Douglas Groothuis, *Revealing the New Age Jesus: Challenges to Orthodox Views of Christ*. Inter-Varsity Press 1990.
Arthur Guirdham, *The Cathars and Reincarnation*. 1970; Turnstone Press edn 1982.

Rosamund E. M. Harding, *An Anatomy of Inspiration*. Heffer 1942.
Arthur Hastings, *With the Tongues of Men and Angels* (Holt Rinehart & Winston 1991); summarized in his article in *Noetic Sciences Review* (Spring/Summer 1991).
Paul Heelas, 'The Sacralization of the Self and New Age Capitalism', in N. Abercrombie and A. Warde, ed., *Social Change in Contemporary Britain*. Polity Press 1991.
John Hick (1), *Death and Eternal Life*. Collins 1976.
John Hick (2), *Evil and the God of Love*. Macmillan 1966.
Aldous Huxley, *The Perennial Philosophy*. Chatto & Windus 1946.

Keith Innes, 'Looking at the New Age', *Anvil* vol. 8, No. 1 (1991), pp. 19–33.
Neil Irwin, *Understanding Crystals*. Aquarian Press 1991.

David and Rebecca Jenkins, *Free to Believe*. BBC Books 1991.
Prudence Jones, *Creative Astrology*. Aquarian Press 1991.
Journal of the American Society for Psychical Research, 5 West 73rd Street, New York, NY 10023, USA.
Journal of Near-Death Studies, Human Sciences Press, 233 Spring Street, New York, NY 10013–1578, USA.
Journal of Parapsychology, PO Box 6847, College Station, Durham, NC 27708, USA.
Journal of Religion and Psychical Research, PO Box 614, Bloomfield, CT 06002, USA.
Journal of the Society for Psychical Research, 49 Marloes Road, London W8 6LA.

Jon Klimo, *Channeling* (Jeremy Tarcher 1987); UK edn, photographically reproduced, under the title *Psychics, Prophets and Mystics*. Aquarian Press 1991.

Dan Korem, *Powers: Testing the Psychic and Supernatural*. Hodder & Stoughton 1989.

Leading Edge, R/O Warwick House, Wells Road, Great Malvern, Worcs., WR14 4RW.

Light, The College of Psychic Studies, 16 Queensberry Place, London SW7 2EB.

Stephen Levine, *Healing into Life and Death*. Anchor/Doubleday 1987.

James R. Lewis, *The New Age Movement: A Bibliography of Conservative Christian Literature*, Santa Barbara Centre, Occasional Paper No. 2, Santa Barbara Centre for Humanistic Studies, PO Box 91611, Santa Barbara, CA 93190–1611, USA.

J. Lindblom, *Prophecy in Ancient Israel*. Blackwell 1962.

Roy Livesey, *More Understanding the New Age*. New Wine Press 1990.

David Lorimer, *Whole in One: The Near-Death Experience and the Ethic of Interconnectedness*. Arkana 1990.

James Lovelock, *Gaia*. Oxford University Press 1982.

T. R. Luhrmann, review of Crowley in *The Christian Parapsychologist*, vol. 8, No. 3 (September 1989), pp. 109–11.

Kevin and Sue McClure, *Stars and Rumours of Stars*. Privately printed 1980, and available from 42 Victoria Road, St Austell, Cornwall PL25 4QD.

Alistair I. McIntosh, 'Psychedelic shamanism: old world to New Age', in *The Christian Parapsychologist*, vol. 6, No. 4 (December 1985), pp. 123–33.

E. L. Mascall and Barbara Jones, *Pi in the High*. Faith Press 1959.

S. L. MacGregor Mathers, *The Kabbalah Unveiled*. Penguin/Arkana 1991, reprinted from the 1926 edn.

Nettie Colburn Maynard in *The ESP Reader*, ed. David C. Knight. Grosset and Dunlap 1969.

J. Gordon Melton (1) *Encyclopaedia of American Religions*, 3rd edn.

J. Gordon Melton (2) with Jerome Clark and Aidan A. Kelly, *New Age Almanac*. Visible Ink Press 1991.

Michael Mitton and Russ Parker, *Requiem Healing*. Darton, Longman & Todd 1991.

Ruth Montgomery, *Strangers Among Us*. Fawcett Crest 1979.

Raymond A. Moody, *Life After Life: The Investigation of a Phenomenon – Survival of Bodily Death*. Mockingbird Books 1975; subsequently a Bantam paperback.

E. Garth Moore, *A Consideration of the Gift of Sensitivity or Mediumship in a Christian Context*. Churches' Fellowship for Psychical and Spiritual Studies.

Melvin Morse with Paul Perry, *Closer to the Light: Learning from the Near-death Experiences of Children*. Villard Books 1991.

Thelma Moss, *The Probability of the Impossible*. Routledge & Kegan Paul 1976/7.

Lesslie Newbigin, in *Christian Uniqueness Reconsidered*, ed. Gavin D'Costa. Orbis Books 1990.

Oliver Nichelson, Guest Editorial in the *Journal of Near-Death Studies*, vol. 8, No. 4 (Summer 1991), p. 204.

Dennis Nineham, review of Uta Ranke-Heinemann, *Eunuchs for Heaven: The Catholic Church and Sexuality*, *Theology*, vol. 94, No. 760 (July/August 1991), p. 313.

Noetic Sciences Review, 475 Gate Five Road, Suite 300, Sausalito, CA 94965, USA.

Ivy Northage (Channelling 'Chan'), 'The Role of the Guide', *Light*, vol. 111, No. 1 (Spring 1991), pp. 21–30.

Jan Opsal, 'Ahmadiyya: Heresy or True Islam?', *Areopagus*, vol. 4, No. 1 (Christmas 1990), pp. 8–10.

Karlis Osis and Erlendur Haraldsson, *At The Hour of Death*. Avon Books 1977.

Helen Palmer, *The Enneagram: Understanding Yourself and the Others in Your Life*. HarperSanFrancisco 1991.

Emily Peach. *Tarot Prediction*. Aquarian Press 1991.

Michael Perry, ed., for the Christian Exorcism Study Group (1) *Deliverance: Psychic Disturbance and Occult Involvement*. SPCK 1987.

Michael Perry (2), 'Method and Model in the Epistle to the Hebrews', *Theology*, vol. 77, No. 644 (February 1974), pp. 66–74.

Michael Perry (3), 'Mystics, Psychics, and Christian Orthodoxy', *The Christian Parapsychologist*, vol. 8, No. 7 (September 1990), pp. 249–57.

Michael Perry (4), *Psychic Studies: A Christian's View*. Aquarian Press 1984.

Michael Perry (5), *The Resurrection of Man*. Mowbray's Library of Theology 1975.

Michael Perry (6), review of Wilson in the *Journal of the Society for Psychical Research*, vol. 51, No. 789 (October 1981), pp. 167–70.

Michael Perry (7), 'Taking Satan Seriously', *The Expository Times*, vol. 101, No. 4 (January 1990), pp. 105–12.

Simone Petrement, *A Separate God: The Christian Origins of Gnosticism*. HarperSanFrancisco 1990.

James A. Pike, *The Other Side*. W. H. Allen 1969.

Judith Pinhey, *The Music of Love*. Collins Fount 1990.

Psychical Studies, the Newsletter of the Unitarian Society for Psychical Studies, Waterbarrow, High Cunsey, Ambleside, Cumbria LA22 0LH.

Quarterly Review of the Churches' Fellowship for Psychical and Spiritual Studies. Address as at note 9 to Chapter 10, above.

April L. Radbill, 'What Spirit Communicators Say About God', *Spiritual Frontiers*, vol. 23, No. 1 (Winter 1991), pp. 27–30; and No. 2 (Spring 1991), pp. 97–103.

Maurice Rawlings, *Beyond Death's Door*. Nashville, Thomas Nelson 1978; London, Sheldon Press 1979.

Carol Riddell, *The Findhorn Community: Creating a Human Identity for the 21st Century*. Findhorn Press 1991.

Jane Ridder-Patrick, *A Handbook of Medical Astrology*. Arkana 1990.

Kenneth Ring (1), *Heading Toward Omega*. William Morrow 1984.

Kenneth Ring (2), *Life at Death*. Coward McCann & Geoghegan 1980.

Kenneth Ring and Christopher Rosing, 'The Omega Project: An Empirical Study of the NDE-Prone Personality', *Journal of Near-Death Studies*, vol. 8, No. 4 (Summer 1990), pp. 211–39.

C. E. Bechhofer Roberts, *The Trial of Mrs Duncan*. Jarrold's Old Bailey Trial Series, No. 3, 1945.

Serena Roney-Dougal, *Where Science and Magic Meet*. Element Books 1991.

J. C. Saavedra-Aguilar and J. S. Gómez-Jeria, 'A Neurobiological Model for Near-Death Experiences', *Journal of Near-Death Studies*, vol. 7, No. 4 (Summer 1989), pp. 205–22.

Elisabeth Sahtouris, *Gaia – the Human Journey*. Pocket Books 1989.

M. Basilea Schlink, *New Age from a Biblical Viewpoint*. Evangelical Sisterhood of Mary, Darmstadt; English trans. published by the Sisterhood, from Radlett, Herts., WD7 8DE.

David Scott, 'Pluralism: Problem or Promise?', *The Evangelical Outlook*, vol. 28, No. 2 (Summer 1991), p. 5.

Philip Seddon, *The New Age – An Assessment*. Grove Spirituality Series No. 34, Grove Books, 1990.

Rupert Sheldrake, *The Rebirth of Nature: The Greening of Science and God*. Century 1990.

Robert Skutch, *Journey Without Distance: The Story Behind A Course in Miracles*. Celestial Arts 1984.

Peter Spink (1) *A Christian in the New Age*. Darton Longman & Todd 1991.

Peter Spink (2) *The End of an Age*. Omega Trust Publications 1983.

Peter Spink (3) *Spiritual Man in a New Age*. Darton Longman & Todd, 1980.

Spiritual Frontiers, PO Box 7868, Philadelphia, PA 19101, USA.

Starhawk, *The Spiral Dance*. Harper & Row 1989.

Ian Stevenson, *Children who Remember Previous Lives: A Question of Reincarnation*. University Press of Virginia 1987. See also his earlier volumes: *Twenty Cases Suggestive of Reincarnation* (American Society for Psychical Research 1966; 2nd edn revised and enlarged, University Press of Virginia 1974); *Cases of the Reincarnation Type* (University Press of Virginia: vol. 1, *Ten Cases in India*, 1975; vol. 2, *Ten Cases in Sri Lanka*, 1977; vol. 3, *Twelve Cases in Lebanon and Turkey*, 1980).

The Story of the White Eagle Lodge. White Eagle Publishing Trust 1986.

Lowell D. Streiker, *New Age Comes to Main Street: What Worried Christians Must Know*. Abingdon Press 1990.

William Stringfellow and Anthony Towne, *The Death and Life of Bishop Pike*. Doubleday 1976.

Linda Tarazi, 'An Unusual Case of Hypnotic Regression With Some Unexplained Contents', *Journal of the American Society for Psychical Research*, vol. 84, No. 4 (October 1990), pp. 309–44.

Charles T. Tart, 'Concerning the Scientific Study of the Human Aura', *Journal of the Society for Psychical Research*, vol. 46, No. 751 (March 1972), pp. 1–21.

Theology, SPCK, Holy Trinity Church, Marylebone Road, London NW1 4DU.

Keith Thomas, *Religion and the Decline of Magic*. Weidenfeld & Nicolson 1971.

Brian Thorne, *Behold the Man*. Darton Longman & Todd 1991.

Christopher Tuckett, reviewing Birger Pearson, *Gnosticism, Judaism and Egyptian Christianity* (Fortress Press 1990), in *The Expository Times*, vol. 102, No. 8 (May 1991), pp. 247–8.

G. N. M. Tyrrell, *The Personality of Man: New Facts and their Significance*. Penguin Books 1947.

John Weldon and Zola Levitt, *Is There Life After Death?* Harvest House Publishers, USA, 1977; Kingsway 1978.

Cedric W. M. Wilson and Michael Perry, 'Deliverance and dowsing', *The Christian Parapsychologist*, vol. 8, No. 5 (March 1990), pp. 195–7.

Ian Wilson, *Mind out of Time?* Victor Gollancz 1981.

Charles C. Wise, Jr., 'Psychical and Mystical Experiences Wedded to Philosophy', *Journal of Religion and Psychical Research*, vol. 11, No. 4 (October 1988), pp. 203–4; vol. 12, No. 1 (January 1989), pp. 39–41; vol.12, No. 2 (April 1989), pp. 96–8.

Roger Woolger, *Other Lives, Other Selves*. US edn, Doubleday 1987; UK edn, Crucible 1990.

Frances Young, *The Making of Creeds*. SCM Press/TPI 1991.

Carol Zaleski, *Otherworld Journeys*. Oxford University Press 1987.

Had the following two titles been published before I had completed the writing of the book I would have used and recommended them:

John Drane, *What is the New Age Saying to the Church?* Marshall Pickering 1991.

Joyce Watson, *A Guide to the New Age for Confused Christians*. Grove Pastoral Series No. 47, Grove Books 1991.

Index